20th Anniversary

YOGA
AND THE PATH OF THE
URBAN MYSTIC

DARREN MAIN

FORWARD BY STEPHEN COPE
Author of *Yoga and the Quest for the True Self*

Dedicated to my mother, Kathy Ascare
and to my father John Main.
Mom, your devotion to me has been unwavering
and your unconditional love has been
my greatest source of strength.
Dad, your honesty and integrity
have been my moral compass along this journey.
Thank you both for making this book
and everything I do possible.

CONTENTS

ENDORSEMENTS

Darren Main's latest book, *Yoga and the Path of the Urban Mystic*, is intended for those facing the quintessential trials of modern life, while simultaneously attempting to live out a spiritual one... Main covers dense territory in a clear, straightforward manner while drawing from ancient texts such as the Bhagavad Gita, the Upanishads and the Yoga Sutra.

—RYAN ALLEN LA YOGA MAGAZINE

Darren Main explains how to turn [life's] distractions into darshan, with humor, lightness and love. He also explains the Yoga Sutra, the chakras, pranayama and other esoteric yoga philosophies in a live and engaging way. His humorous style and delicious honesty create a thoroughly modern approach to this ancient science.

—THE BODHI TREE REVIEW

Darren Main is wonderfully talented at bringing the essence of living yoga off the mat fully to life for all who are on the yoga path. He writes in a friendly and accessible tone that makes often esoteric philosophical concepts easy to grasp in practical ways that one can apply in daily life. I highly recommend this book to all yoga students and teachers interested in more deeply exploring the practice on the mat and bringing it all more broadly into their life out in the larger world.

—MARK STEPHENS
Author of *Teaching Yoga: Essential Foundations and Techniques*

With gentle humor and obvious knowledge, Darren Main shares with us his practice and understanding of yoga. He does a beautiful job of interspersing his life experiences with the classical teachings in a way that makes them clear and alive. You will enjoy this book.

—JUDITH HANSON LASATER, Ph.D.
Author of *30 Essential Yoga Poses and Living Your Yoga*

Darren Main takes yoga off the yoga mat—adroitly applying the ancient system of yoga to the daily challenges of the modern mystic. Combining personal insight and anecdotes with practical, down-to-earth teachings, he brings you into a world in which every part of your life has sacred and transformative potential

—YOGI AMRIT DESAI
Founder of Kripalu Yoga, Lenox, MA, and author of *Amrit Yoga*

In *Yoga and the Path of the Urban Mystic* Darren Main has given us a wonderful doorway into the potentially complex world of raja yoga. His work provides us with a compelling but accessible Baedeker to the sometimes dense world of Indian metaphysics. It is a yoga commentary with a uniquely American voice. It is piquant, experience-near, real, contemporary, and very sensitive to the reader for whom the world of Sanskrit terms and Indian ideas is completely new and foreign. Darren's work, like raja yoga itself, is precise and methodical in its approach to spiritual practice.

—STEPHEN COPE
Author of *Yoga and the Quest for the True Self*

In *Yoga and The Path Of The Urban Mystic* Darren Main guides his readers to the most precious gift of all—the gift of living a conscious and peaceful life. As the challenge to live an authentic life increases, Darren's timely message makes available the skills needed to deeply listen to our heart's most sincere wisdom and desires. His examples and stories are both candid and loving, and shed just enough light on the mystical path so that each of us might discover our next step towards greater ease and freedom.

—JONATHAN REYNOLDS
Author of *Learning To Listen: Simplifying Spiritual Practice*

Yoga and the Path of the Urban Mystic is the perfect road map for every yoga practitioner who seeks to integrate their practice into every aspect of their lives. It is a warm, funny, practical, inspirational and highly authentic book filled with knowledge, wisdom and history. I recommend it to all of my students wholeheartedly and with joy. I am very grateful for what Darren Main has given the world through the birth of this book.

—CHRISTINE BURKE
Director, Liberation Yoga, Los Angeles, CA

Darren brings ancient wisdom to life in his *Yoga and the Path of the Urban Mystic*. Filled with fascinating information and inspiring stories that help us realize how we can uniquely apply these yogic principles to our modern lives, this book offers great inspiration and encouragement.

—KIM WATERS
Illustrator of Illuminations from the Bhagavad Gita, lead singer of 'Rasa'

Darren is a beautiful bright soul who has a very grounded and practical way of presenting the teachings of Yoga to Westerners.

—CLAYTON HORTON
Director, Greenpath Yoga Studio, San Francisco, CA.

Darren Main uses engaging real people stories, authentic sacred texts and lively spiritual discourse to create a 21 st century guide to yoga. *Yoga and the Path of the Urban Mystic* takes the ancient melody of yoga and inserts the beat of modern life. It is something we all should dance to.

—ELISE MARIE COLLINS
Author of *An A-Z Guide to Healing Foods & Chakra Tonics*

Yoga and the Path of the Urban Mystic is an insightful, down-to-earth, and user-friendly introduction to the mystical path of yoga. I especially enjoyed reading Darren's personal experiences and anecdotes which beautifully describe the process of transformation on and off the mat.

—TODD NORIAN
International Yoga Instructor

A practical, easy-to-read road map to becoming an Urban Mystic

—GERALD G. JAMPOLSKY, M.D.
Author of *Shortcuts to God and Love is Letting Go of Fear*

As hatha yoga finds itself ever more popular, *Yoga and the Path of the Urban Mystic* helps to move our practice off the mat and into our modern day lives, in a way that is simple, yet filled with profound wisdom. This book inspires joy (samadhi).

—TARA DALE
Founder of Yoga Tree, San Francisco, CA

Darren Main has constructed a wonderfully accessible guidebook for the spiritual traveler. For anyone beginning their journey on the path that winds between the spiritual and the secular, between the mystical and the mundane, *Yoga and the Path of the Urban Mystic* offers the basic tenets of yoga as guide posts. For someone who is not ready to begin cave dwelling and self-inflicted asceticism, Darren has managed to condense very complicated principles into tangible and applicable tenets for living a spiritual life in our complicated and challenging urban world.

—DR. ARIEL COYOTE
Cofounder of Open Door Yoga, San Francisco, CA

In his book *Yoga and the Path of the Urban Mystic*, Darren Main gives insight into ancient yogic teachings, which continue to shed light in today's world. Stories are told in simple terms which are easy to grasp and understand. Darren also shares personal examples from his own life experiences, which demonstrate how to embrace the philosophy and practice of yoga from a modern perspective. This delightful book offers inspiration for staying spiritually centered in contemporary times.

—**ANNALISA CUNNINGHAM**
Author of *Yoga Vacations and Spa Vacations*

Darren has translated most of the ancient and classical Sanskrit terms of spiritual practice into a modern jargon around his idea of being an Urban Mystic. He then sprinkles these descriptions with delightful examples from his own journey of "walking his talk" in his daily yoga practice. Very down to earth advice for open readers!

—**SATYAM NADEEN**
Author of *From Onions to Pearls and From Seekers to Finders*

Darren Main's teaching represents the true essence of yoga. Humble and honest— you will not find a more real and grounded teacher. For this, Darren has gained much respect in the yoga world.

—**MICHAEL WATSON**
Director, Bermuda Health Coop, Bermuda

It has been said that what makes a great teacher is not only the message, but the ability to convey it to the student. In the case of *Yoga and the Path of the Urban Mystic*, Main has bravely and adeptly shared with us the essence of the great message of yoga. In simple, yet meaningfully written language he shares his insights, sometimes baring parts of his own struggles along the path. The result is a work that embraces the human experience and lends understanding and compassion to all who seek yoga's gifts.

—**CHRISTOPHER LOVE**
Yoga Instructor, San Francisco, CA

Yoga and the Path of the Urban Mystic is a delightful introspective into the hearts and minds of humankind. Darren Main offers a unique exploration of the science of yoga that is extremely in-depth and filled with insight. I thoroughly enjoyed this book.

—BETSY JONES
Director of Hot Yoga Louisville, Louisville, Kentucky

Darren is a very popular guest teacher at our studio. He shares yoga philosophy in a way that appeals to students and teachers alike. His asana classes exude humor, a love for yoga and a strong passion for the practice as a whole. Darren is fluent in a variety of topics that convey a non-dogmatic approach to the practice of yoga.

—KIMBERLY WILSON
Author of *Tranquilista: Mastering the Art of Enlightened Work and Mindful Play*

Kristin Olson's Urban Yoga Center has long supported Darren and his yoga style, his writings of the path of the enlightened searcher. The Urban Mystic is accessible to anyone, entertaining and a wonderful personal story of Darren's curiosity, his searching and pondering of his experiences in this lifetime. Good for anyone and everyone with a passion and a full breath, this is a gift for the heart.

—KRISTIN OLSON
Director, Urban Yoga, Palm Springs, CA

In *Yoga and the Path of the Urban Mystic*, Darren Main offers incredible insight into how to apply yogic philosophy to our modern, western lives. Through his words, the reader relates to him and feels at ease with the 'struggle' to integrate "the spiritual" into earthly life. Darren presents yoga in a way that is user friendly and in a non-threatening manner to the reader, thus making it more accessible to a larger audience. I am proud and honored to have Darren as a colleague.

—AARON STAR
Founder of Blue Osa Yoga Center & Spa, Costa Rica

HATHA YOGA PRAYER

I offer this practice to the Sadguru,
the Teacher within all things,
The Teacher that is the Prana (life)
from which my body emerged,
The Teacher that sustains
and nourishes me with each breath.
The Teacher whose lessons
are in every life experience—even pain and death.

May this practice open me to the wisdom of the Sadguru,
that my mind may know peace,
that my heart may know compassion,
And my life may offer peace and compassion to all beings.
Om Shanti, Om Peace

—DARREN MAIN

FOREWORD BY STEPHEN COPE

In the summer of 1893, a young Indian Swami electrified American audiences at the First World Parliament of Religions with his discourses about "the Science of Yoga." The 29-year-old Swami Vivekananda, whose arrival at Chicago's Columbian exposition was cloaked in mystery, held audiences of 7,000 spellbound with his descriptions of "the fully alive human being"—or jiva mukti, "the soul awake in this lifetime." Yogis, he said, had discovered that all human beings have astonishing potentials of mind, body, and spirit—potentials that can be awakened through the practical science of liberation, which he described in his talks.

Vivekananda quickly became American's first yoga celebrity. After his triumph in Chicago, he traveled extensively around the United States, teaching the systematic path of awakening which he called "raja yoga." Raja yoga, he claimed, "is the epitome of all yoga psychology"—combining all of the different schools of yogic practice, devotion (bhakti yoga), selfless service (karma yoga), the yoga of intellectual refinement (jnana yoga), and the yoga of postures and breathing (hatha yoga), into a methodical psycho-spiritual technology which is guaranteed to transform the human character, energy system and consciousness. "Raja yoga is," he claimed, "an exact science."

On that summer morning in Chicago, Vivekananda opened the door to yoga in America. Since that time, dozens of Indian yoga adepts have walked through it—most of them with a message very similar to Vivekananda's: all human beings have the potential to wake up in this lifetime, to become fully alive human beings.

Over a century later, yoga has taken America by storm. Recent surveys suggest that as many as 20 million Americans are now involved in some aspect of the practice of yoga—in health clubs, YMCA's, yoga centers, and private living rooms around the country. Not surprisingly, America's first wave of enthusiasm for this ancient practice has centered around the practices of yoga postures (asana) and breathing exercises (pranayama). But thousands of American yogis have now begun to discover that these practices are inextricably linked to the entire science of transformation described by the young traveling swami over a century ago.

As Americans inevitably begin to lift the lid of Vivekananda's methodical science of liberation, many will find that it has great appeal. It's practical. It's non-religious. And, most importantly, it doesn't require retreat from the world. Quite the opposite: Yoga psychology transforms the most mundane activities of daily life into spiritual practices. The way we eat, breathe, move, dream, have sex, speak, work, all become opportunities for transformation and development.

In *Yoga and the Path of the Urban Mystic*, Darren Main has given us a wonderful doorway into the potentially complex world of raja yoga. His work provides us with a compelling but accessible Baedeker to the sometimes-dense world of Indian metaphysics. It is a yoga commentary with a uniquely American voice. It is piquant, experience-near, real, contemporary and very sensitive to the reader for whom the world of Sanskrit terms and Indian ideas is completely new and foreign. Darren's work, like raja yoga itself, is precise and methodical in its approach to spiritual practice.

Yoga and the Path of the Urban Mystic is a welcome contribution to the burgeoning American literature on yoga—a contemporary story that will help to take the views and practices of yoga more deeply into the journey initiated so many years ago by the visionary young Swami.

—STEPHEN COPE
Lenox, Massachusetts

Stephen Cope is the author of *Yoga and the Quest for the True Self* and *The Wisdom of Yoga: A Seeker's Guide to Extraordinary Living*. He is the Scholar in Residence at the Kripalu Center for Yoga and Health in Lenox, Massachusetts.

AUTHOR'S NOTE

Throughout this book I make reference to various individuals within the context of stories and examples. While I have based these stories on real people and real situations, I have changed many of the names, circumstances and details of each story in an effort to respect the privacy of the individuals involved. In the few cases where I have not changed the identity of a person, I have obtained their permission or found mention of these persons and events within the public record.

TRANSLATION OF SACRED TEXTS

Throughout this book, I quote a number of sacred texts from India. There are many wonderful translations of these texts available, each with its own perspective and wisdom. For consistency, I have chosen to quote from translations that will be most clear for the modern yogi. I would like to thank the following authors and publisher for allowing me to reprint small sections of their translations throughout this book.

The Bhagavad Gita Translated by Eknath Easwaran Nilgiri Press
©1985 • www.nilgiri.org

The Upanishads Translated by Eknath Easwaran Nilgiri Press
©1987 • www.nilgiri.org

The Yoga Sutra of Patanjali Translated by Chip Hartranft
Shambhala Publications
© 2002 • www.shambhala.com

The Hatha Yoga Pradipika Translated by Brian Dana Akers
YogaVidya
© 2002 • www.yogavidya.com

The Gheranda Samhita Translated by James Mallinson YogaVidya
© 2004 • www.yogavidya.com

The Shiva Samhita Translated by James Mallinson Yoga Vidya
© 2007 • www.yogavidya.com

INTRODUCTION

"Those who aspire to the state of yoga
should seek the self in inner solitude."
—BHAGAVAD GITA, 6:10

At 5:30 each morning, my stereo is programmed to wake me up. This morning I awoke to the soft sound of Krishna Das chanting his "Devi Puja." As the deep, rich sound of Krishna Das' voice coaxed me out of a dream I couldn't quite remember and into a waking state, I considered going back to sleep and skipping my morning practice altogether. Yet something deep within pulled me out of bed.

This morning was not much different from other mornings. I put on some water for tea and lit a few candles and an aromatherapy lamp. My small bedroom was magically transformed into a sacred temple. It was chilly, so I turned on the heat and sipped on some hot herbal tea while I washed my face, brushed my teeth and slipped into the loose-fitting, white cotton clothes that I reserve for my spiritual practice. Finally, I rolled out my yoga mat and began.

I started my practice by bowing my head to the earth in surrender and chanting a devotional prayer, followed by the sound of "Om." I then entered into some yogic breathing techniques. My mind and body began to wake up. Before long I was in downward-dog pose. I have done this pose a few thousand times, yet still my body resisted it. Again I considered going back to bed, but instead chose to breathe more deeply. After a few more yoga poses, my body and mind began to melt into the practice. My resistance faded, and I felt my whole being entering into an effortless rhythm, holding some poses and flowing through others—each pose bringing me deeper and deeper into the practice. I moved from downward-dog to upward-dog and then hopped through to assume triangle pose.

My breath was shallow at times, and when I realized this I allowed it to deepen, filling my entire body. I finished my asana (poses) practice by moving through a series of floor poses that included the camel, the cobra and the posterior stretch. After doing several rounds of the 'breath of fire,' I took a seat on my meditation cushion, wrapped myself in a white blanket, and closed my eyes. Now my breath was deep, but unregulated. I felt my mind resting on the breath, but often drifting into plans for my day. Each time I noticed myself playing this familiar game, I smiled and returned my mind to the gentle flow of my breath. I sat for what felt like both an eternity and a few short moments. I opened my eyes softly and concluded my morning practice with a brief reading from the Upanishads and then chanted the sound of 'Om.'

As I rose from my meditation cushion I could feel a quiet calm. I showered, dressed, and walked down to Courtney's, a small corner market that is famous in San Francisco. My goal was simple—to buy some fresh fruit and yogurt for breakfast. As I waited for the light to change, I took a few deep breaths. Children were showing up at the grade school across from my home. I felt as though nothing could shake my peace of mind...but in the moment that followed that thought, I stepped out into the street, only to hear the blare of a car horn. A woman in a tiny car ran the red light and nearly knocked me over. To add insult to injury, she gave me the finger.

I was flustered, but continued across the street to the market, only to find that they were out of yogurt. I begrudgingly settled for some granola and rice milk. On the way home I picked up the morning paper and began to read the headlines as I walked. I read that the economy was still showing signs of slowing, and that another teen had shot his classmates somewhere near San Diego.

By the time I got home again, less than one city block, I could feel stress consuming my body and mind. As I walked by my bedroom door I caught the scent of lavender from my aromatherapy lamp. I had to laugh! Not more than an hour earlier, I was sitting in peace, and here I was now, in the middle of a drama that my ego and the environment had conspired to create.

This, of course, is the difficulty in trying to live a deeply spiritual and centered life. It is why most people who really want to cultivate a life that is devoted to and guided by Spirit consider renouncing

the world to find a quiet little cave or monastery. The world we have created is not one that encourages a spiritual life. Therefore, it is challenging to try to live as an urban mystic. Nothing short of a deeply held commitment will suffice. That is what this book is all about.

I use the term urban mystic because it describes a great many of us. A mystic is a person, from any spiritual tradition, who seeks an intimate relationship with Spirit. A mystic may or not be a religious person, but he or she is committed to turning his or her mind over to the guidance of Spirit. A mystic seeks a direct experience of the Divine, but mysticism is not to be confused with religion, for religions seek to explain what cannot be explained, and a mystic seeks to know through experience.

In the past, people who wanted to practice mysticism would go off to a hermitage or join a religious order. Some were revered, others seen as fools. In either case they did not fit into the worldly life. They saw things through very different eyes, and as a result they did not have a home in the urban world.

This is all starting to change. People from all walks of life are developing a deeper connection to Spirit and living in the world at the same time. They are meditating on their lunch breaks and practicing Tai Chi before the kids get up. These urban mystics are filling yoga classes and studying kabala. There is a movement underway, and it is much more than a flaky New Age fad. People are looking for something more than a good job, a sexy spouse and some over-inflated stock options.

Sitting next to my computer is a statue of the Buddha. He has a shaved head and is wrapped in a saffron robe. His legs wind gently into a lotus pose and his eyes are softly closed in meditation. In one hand he holds a cellular phone and in the other a cup of coffee. I keep this little statue by my computer because it reminds me so much of the spiritual path I am on. Like many others, I am called, or so it would seem, to walk between two worlds. I am torn between living a deeply contemplative life and being a full-fledged member of my secular community.

There are a growing number of people in our western culture and around the globe who are torn between two worlds. On the one hand we strive to grow spiritually and to seek the deeper meaning of life. We yearn to know the secrets of Spirit, and we know what needs to be done to make the earth a peaceful place. On the other hand, we feel a need to live in communities and contribute to society.

The problem is not in our commitment, for that is very strong. The problem is that we are torn. Many spiritual techniques, yoga included, were developed by and for people who had renounced the world. Rather than form families, build homes and live in the community, the mystics responsible for such techniques as yoga and kabala left the material world and went to live as monks or nuns.

There are great spiritual lessons to be learned from living in a cloistered setting and stepping outside the basic chores of day-to-day life. Yet there are an equal number, and some would argue more, spiritual benefits and lessons to be gleaned from a secular life. As we begin to walk with one foot on the path of the renunciant and the other on the path of the householder, difficulties arise, and there are not, as yet, mechanisms in place to guide us along. Humanity is evolving into a new level of spiritual awareness, and we are blazing new trails even as I write these words.

────────────── **A B O U T   T H I S   B O O K** ──────────────

As I have practiced yoga in the quest for inner peace, I have found that my spiritual practice doesn't end when I leave the yoga mat or finish my meditation. That is the beginning. While having a time of quiet each day is essential for our spiritual health, it is what we do in the world that propels us forward as individuals and as a society.

Applying the principles of yoga to the whole of life is the key to living as an urban mystic. Sitting in stillness in a quiet room filled with candles is wonderful, but it will not do much good if you're robbed of the peace you so diligently sought in your practice by the first car horn you hear or the daily headlines you read. Yoga can teach you to maintain your communication to Spirit despite the challenges of urban life.

In this book I do not intend to explain God. There are enough books out there attempting to do that. The aim of this book is to outline the life of the urban mystic by using the principles of yoga. It is my hope that I'll be able to make some of the universal principles of mysticism more accessible to the seeker who has a deep desire to connect with Truth and yet feels inspired to live in the 'real' world.

I cannot take credit for this idea, however. The really great teachers have all been in agreement on this. Jesus took the hidden meanings of the Law of Moses and made them user-friendly for the common people of his time. (Matthew 5:17)

Five hundred years before that, Gautama the Buddha spoke of the 'middle path' (madhyamapratipada), which runs between asceticism and secularism. In the The Bhagavad Gita, Krishna spoke of service in the world as being a higher form of praise than living a renunciant's life. Today this idea is being rediscovered, and it is very exciting.

Because many of us have been raised in Western culture, a lot of the ideas yoga presents can be quite foreign. When you combine these cultural differences with the fact that yoga was originally designed for people who had removed themselves from society, many people who are new to yoga can feel overwhelmed.

Therefore, I think it's important to explore some of these new ideas so that the practice of yoga will become more meaningful. In Part One of this book we will be exploring some of the basic tenets of yogic philosophy.

In Part Two, we will be exploring the practice of yoga as outlined by Patanjali in the Yoga Sutra. In addition to bringing a greater understanding to the practice of yoga, we will look at ways in which we can apply that practice to life.

The one thing that is purposely omitted from this book is technique. There are many great books out there that seek to teach proper alignment and poses, breathing techniques, and various forms of seated meditation. It doesn't matter which style of yoga you practice, be it Ashtanga, Iyengar, Kripalu, or some other form.

This book is not a replacement for the style of yoga you feel called to practice. Rather, I hope it will be a complement.

—— **YOGA AS A MYSTICAL PATH** ——

In the past few years, hatha yoga has grown so fast in popularity that many yoga studios are bursting at the seams. By its physical benefits alone, yoga was destined to gain a lot of notoriety, but it would fade into the background if it didn't evolve with the needs of its students. Yoga mats could find a home in that same closet that stores old aerobics videos and mini trampolines. Yoga is a living practice, and things that live must evolve or they become extinct.

Yoga is a 4,000-year-old practice that developed in India at around the same time the Hindu faith was forming. It is not a religion, but rather a science. It provides its practitioners with a proven set of techniques for Self-realization, but it doesn't push a belief. A yogi can be Jewish or Christian, Pagan or Buddhist, agnostic or atheist. Personal beliefs will not change the effectiveness of the yoga practice. In other words, if you practice yoga, you will spiritually open your heart, mind and body. Nothing more is needed than your commitment to the practice.

The word yoga means 'union' in Sanskrit. This union includes a realization of the oneness between the mind and body as well as between them and the soul and Spirit. A yogi seeks a direct experience of oneness with Spirit by letting go of all the things being held between conscious mind and Spirit. Many people associate yoga with the physical poses that make up hatha yoga, but yoga is a more comprehensive practice than simply stretching and breathing. In fact, many styles of yoga pay little attention to the poses and breathing, and focus more on meditation.

Like many spiritual traditions, yoga was handed down verbally from teacher to student for many generations. It's difficult to pinpoint when or how it all got started, but it began to solidify when a great Indian sage named Patanjali decided to write down the principles of yoga in what is now called The Yoga Sutra, some 1800 years ago.

The Yoga Sutra is not long, less than 200 short verses that outline the principles of yoga in a very open and indeterminable way. There is an amazing amount of room in which to interpret these verses, and as a result, there are widely differing styles and traditions of yoga. In addition to the Yoga Sutra, yoga draws on numerous other texts, including the Vedas, Upanishads, Bhagavad Gita, The Tantric texts, The Hatha Yoga Pradipika, The Gheranda Samhita and The Shiva Samhita to name just a few.

Modern yoga looks much different than it did when Patanjali was scribing his Yoga Sutra, but the backbone that makes yoga such an effective practice still exists. It is my hope that this book will help you move your experience of yoga off the yoga mat and meditation cushion and into the whole of life. By doing this, the life of the urban mystic comes very much within reach.

——————— ONE LAST THOUGHT ———————

Remember that yoga, like all mystical traditions, is a practice, not perfection. It's the process of returning to your yoga practice over and over again that gives you the benefits. Doing the perfect yoga pose or clearing your mind of all thought is well and good, but in the end it is the practice of returning to yoga that allows you to live life to the fullest.

Car horns will continue to distract you; the drama of your ego and your external environment will pull your mind far from the practice of yoga, but eventually you will return. That is how it works. Try to let go of the idea that you need to do yoga perfectly to see its benefits and learn to enjoy the process of waking to a deeper understanding of who you really are. By doing this, you will know joy, and that joy will be your gift to a world that very much needs our healing.

Namaste,

Darren

www.darrenmain.com

---

*"The practitioner will succeed;
the non-practitioner will not.
Success in yoga is not achieved
by merely reading books."*

—HATHA YOGA PRADIPIKA 1:65

PART ONE

"The entire universe is the creation of thought.
The play of the mind is just a creation of thought.
Abandon the mind which is only thought.
Take refuge in the changeless...
and surely find peace."

—HATHA YOGA PRADIPIKA 4:58

CHAPTER ONE

Atman
and the
Ego

"Beyond all attributes, the supreme Self is the eternal witness, ever pure, indivisible, and uncompounded. Far beyond the ego. In him conflicts and expectations cease."
—ATMA UPANISHAD 1:5

THE SELF

"The Supreme Self is neither born nor dies. He cannot be burned, moved, pierced, cut nor dried. Beyond all attributes, the supreme Self is eternal witness, ever pure, indivisible and uncompounded, far beyond the senses and the ego."
—ATMA UPANISHAD

I was at my brother's wedding several months ago, and I met a beautiful young lady. Her name is Megan, and she immediately came up to me and asked me to be her boyfriend. She had a radiant spirit, and a smile that was more contagious than chicken pox.

Most people dream of marrying a person like Megan—someone who is overflowing with positive energy and enthusiasm. But for as open and sweet as Megan is, there was a little catch. Megan was six years old—much too young to start dating, and by the time she is old enough, the world will have whispered all sorts of misinformation in her ears.

We all start out with Megan's joy and enthusiasm for life, but somewhere along the line it all gets muddled, and we forget who we are. We start to see ourselves as needing to fight to get by, and needing to make the grade to establish our worth. As we become adults, we become more and more fixated on the drama of our lives, and we lose sight of our true natures. The simplicity and joy of childhood get stamped out, and we maintain only a vague memory of the innocence and freedom that once characterized us. While we never lose our capacity for joy, we do forget, and it is this forgotten identity that hangs around us like a heavy weight. This is why a person can so often feel like a tiny mouse trapped under a heavy carpet with nowhere to move and nothing left to do except wait to die.

This forgotten identity stems from the very popular notion that we need to be fixed—that somehow, there is something wrong with us. Perhaps we are told that we are born with 'original sin', or maybe we are told that we have to fight to succeed in the world. But whatever form this lie takes, most of us live our lives as if this lie were the only thing in this world that is actually true. It seems to be a given that there will be winners and losers and that we will wind up with either the 'haves' or the 'have-nots'.

At its core, yoga has the sole goal of returning our minds to the state of innocence we were created with. While many people embark on their yoga journeys for the physical benefits, the real reward comes when we let go of our day-to-day drama, and remember who we are.

When I first met Megan at my brother's wedding, I smiled and asked her if she knew that the name Megan meant 'warrior princess' in Swahili. Her eyes lit up and she clapped her hands.

"Does that make me a warrior princess?" she asked.

"I don't know. What do you think?" I said. She started laughing and hopping up and down and then ran over to her mom and dad to inform them that they had a warrior princess for a daughter.

There was a woman next to me who was unimpressed and tried to bait me into an argument; she asked me if I knew how to speak Swahili fluently or if I simply knew a few words. When I admitted that I had no idea what the word 'Megan' meant in Swahili and that I was just telling Megan a little story, she gave me a very disgusted look.

"You need to go over there and tell her the truth. That poor little girl is going to go through life believing that she is a warrior princess," the woman snapped.

"But she is a warrior princess," I replied. "And if I were to tell her anything to the contrary, I would be encouraging her to forget just how wonderful she is."

Of course the sacred texts of India don't use the term 'warrior princess' to describe the human soul, but the idea is very present. In the East, the term is Atman and it literally means, "spark of the divine." Atman is the nature and substance of who we are. Buried beneath baggage from our past and fears about the future is Atman. Atman is far beyond our episodes of sickness and health; it is transcendent of jobs, relationships and social status. It's our true Self, and as the passage from the Upanishad states: it cannot be destroyed, or lost— only forgotten.

Paramahansa Yogananda, author of Autobiography of a Yogi, had this to say: "Is a diamond less valuable because it is covered with mud? God sees the changeless beauty of our souls; He knows we are not our mistakes."

The whole practice of yoga is the process of removing the mud from our 'diamond'. This is why a yogi is not trying to get into heaven or find enlightenment. Rather, in yoga, we are trying to realize the peace and contentment that are always present when we gently remove the 'mud' that we think we are and begin to recognize the innate value of our Self—Atman.

This concept is so basic to yoga that to overstate its importance would be impossible. The path of the yogi doesn't lead to a location, but rather to a realization. As a yogi, one doesn't achieve samadhi (ecstasy) by doing good deeds or by perfecting a headstand. He or she finds the peace that is often so elusive by quieting the mind long enough to realize that what was searched for high and low is right there in front of our eyes.

—————— THE NATURE OF ATMAN ——————

"One man believes he is the slayer, another believes he is the slain. Both are ignorant; there is neither slayer nor slain. You were never born; you will never die. You have never changed, you can never change."
—BHAGAVAD GITA 2:19-20

The Self cannot be changed or lost or corrupted. We are like water, which can take many forms, but will always be water. You can boil it, freeze it, or make it murky with impurities, but its essential nature does not change. Water is H 2 O regardless of what form it seems to take. We are Atman whether we play the role of saint or sinner, healthy or sick, rich or poor, happy or unhappy. The form we take doesn't change the nature of who we are.

Because Atman is the spark of the Divine, it shares the same qualities as the Divine. In much the same way that we can be unique individuals and still hold the same genetic qualities as our biological parents, we share the spiritual equivalent of a genetic likeness with the Divine. I can no more stop being a 'child of God' than I can stop being the progeny of my biological parents. The only thing in question is the decision to embrace or deny this spiritual bloodline.

So if we share divine qualities with God, then it would be a good idea to know what those qualities are. First, like God, we are eternal in nature. This is to say that there was never a time when we didn't exist and there will never be a time when we don't exist. In other words we did not begin at our physical birth, and we will not end with our physical death. Atman, our very essence, is timeless.

Second, we are infinite. Many of us tend to think of infinity as a really big number or a really big space, but like eternity, it is much bigger than our time/space perceptions. Infinity is everywhere—and then some. To say that Atman is infinite is to say that there is no place where you are not.

Not only are we eternal and infinite, but also, like God, we are unified. This is to say that there is no separation in our true nature. The Atman within me is also the Atman within you and so on. God is not a bunch of little parts, God is one, and therefore so are we. We sense and experience separation as we look at our world, and we even feel it within our own bodies, but when we begin to experience Atman, we will let all this separateness fall away and experience the oneness of Spirit.

Of course, these three qualities don't seem to apply to us as human beings. You can easily say, "I am not eternal because I am going to die someday." You can also put down this book to walk across the room and thus prove that you're not infinite because you were once there and are now here, and everyone knows that you can't be in two places at once. Or we can also easily prove separation because my body is separate from your body, and my thoughts are different from your thoughts.

Sadly, this is very much what we experience as we walk through the world. By identifying ourselves with our bodies, we 'prove' that we are something we are not. Virtually every relationship we have ever had and every act we have ever done has had the deep-rooted purpose of denying who we are and cloaking Atman from our perception. Why this should be so is discussed in the section on the ego, which follows, and also in Chapter Four, "Karma Yoga and Relationships as a Spiritual Practice."

When we come to the yoga mat, we remind ourselves that the body is an expression of Atman, but not a replacement for it. This opens up the space where healing can happen on all levels of our being, and we can return to that balanced place where we realize our value, worth and completeness as Atman.

Authors Note: When the word Self is capitalized, it represents our eternal divine nature. When it appears in lower case letters, it represents the ego or small self.

THE EGO

"As long as we think we are the ego, we feel attached and fall into sorrow. But realize you are the Self, the Lord of Life, and you will be freed from sorrow."

—MUNDAKA UPANISHAD

The word yoga means 'yoke' or 'union.' It is therefore the practice of bringing together that which is separate, or more accurately, the realization that there is no separation, only oneness and unity. This is no small task, because everything we believe to be true is built on the basic notion of separation. We seem to break things into categories in order to understand them, but really this is the ego making sure that we never see the whole picture. We see our bodies as separate from our minds and emotions, and even our bodies are seen as having separate systems and parts. We see external differences everywhere we look. There are different skin colors and different religions. We see different genders and sexual orientations. There are different classes of people, such as rich and poor, upper class and middle class. Separation abounds in our human experience.

This goes much deeper than many understand. It has become our entire identity, and while it is a false identity, we cling to it with desperate and clutching hands because it is the only reality we seem to know. Of course this flies in the face of our true nature as Atman, but smallness and separateness seem unavoidable truths in this world.

This belief in separation has become our new identity or self. It is the self that we believe we are rather than the Self that we were created to be. This false self is what is known as the ego or ahamkara. It is the source of all suffering.

The ego is nothing more than a false belief—the ultimate lie. It is a mistaken identity—the belief that we are something we are not. It is the denial of our eternal, infinite and unified nature, and it spares no effort to maintain the illusion that we are temporal, finite and separate. It's the core belief that we are not who we were created to be.

Although we are Atman, and joy is our natural birthright, the ego needs to defend against this experience at all costs. It realizes, however dimly, that it would be out of a job very quickly if we sat still long enough to realize our true identities and the power, freedom and ecstasy that come with them.

This is why we get so easily distracted from spiritual practice and healthy living. The ego loves it when we do self-destructive and mindless things; in fact it willfully seeks them out. It wants us to smoke, eat junk food and sit in front of the TV, because as long as we do that, we will surely not remember who we are. This is why living a spiritual and mindful life is so difficult.

About a year ago, I was walking down the street with my friend Jasper. Within the time it took us to walk two blocks, I bumped into three different yoga students I had not seen in awhile. Each of them peppered me with excuses as to why they had not been in class. Each had all sorts of reasons why life was somehow preventing them from maintaining a regular practice. After the third one left, Jasper looked at me and smiled as he said,

"Man, you inspire more guilt than a Catholic nun."

It's not that I try to inspire guilt in my students, of course. That would only fuel the problem, for guilt is the ego's best friend. But my students, when faced with seeing their teacher, are confronted with the fact that they have chosen to fill their hours and days with things that help them to forget their true nature, rather than things to help them quiet the mind and remember Atman.

I am no different from my students. I often find myself eating food that makes me feel heavy, or dating people I don't find stimulating. I easily get distracted by work, Hollywood and the drama of current affairs. I forget to practice more often than I would like to admit.

If I'm not careful, I can easily fall into guilt and self-judgment, and my ego goes crazy, filling my head with thoughts like: "Who are you to be teaching yoga? You can't even practice consistently yourself. Who are you to be giving talks on spirituality and writing books on how to live a more centered life? Your life is a mess!"

Of course this serves nothing but my ego, which delights in my fits of guilt. Through my yoga practice, I have learned to stop those thoughts sooner and sooner. I find that when I do, I quietly return to my breath and then to my meditation cushion or my yoga mat. But as long as I stay in guilt and make up excuses for staying stuck, I find my diet continues to decline, my yoga practice gets weaker, and my mind dips deeper and deeper into the ego's drama.

The key to moving beyond the ego's guilt-based perceptions is not through more guilt, but rather through letting go of guilt. As a modern yogi, the key to finding peace through yoga is to keep coming back to the practice. It doesn't matter how often we get distracted by the ego, or for how long we play the ego's game. The only thing that matters is that we return. Eventually the pain of living under the ego's rule will wear down even the most stubborn person. I am living proof of this. Surrender is inevitable, but the road between guilt and surrender can be long and painful. Developing a solid spiritual practice is a detour around many of the potholes along the way.

It's important to note that the ego is not bad; the ego is simply nothing. It's a poor investment of our time and energy, for everything the ego values will die and return to dust. This is as true of the things we see as temporary (such as the note of a musical instrument which rises and fades as quickly as it is played) as it is of the things we see as long lasting (such as mountains and oceans and stars). All of them will arise out of the nothingness and then, in time, dissolve into the emptiness from which they came.

The ego attaches its value to form, which must change. Atman simply is. It identifies only with the limitless and thus does not produce grief or suffering. When Jesus said, "No man can serve two masters," he was conveying this same truth. As long as you obey the perceptions of your ego, you will not know peace, and as soon as you experience Atman radiating from within, your suffering will become incomprehensible.

THE SEARCH

"Like two golden birds perched on the selfsame tree, intimate friends, the ego and the Self dwell in the same body. The former eats the sweet and sour fruits of the tree of life while the other looks on in detachment."
—MUNDAKA UPANISHAD III 2:1

Our minds are literally split in half, with the eternal Self or Atman existing in a state of pure bliss and unity, and the ego self believing that we are completely separate and vulnerable. This is the cause of much mental anguish, which then leads to emotional and physical suffering, because our ego mind, which is what we identify with most often, feels the need to defend itself against the notion of Atman. When you allow your mind to dwell in the infinite realm of Atman, the ego disappears into the nothingness that it is.

On some level we know our true identities. We know the vastness and the incorruptibility of our true natures and, believing that we are egos, we grieve at that loss. Although this grief is largely unconscious, it motivates most of our actions and reactions in this world. On some level we know there is more to life, but finding out what it is seems so elusive. We have tricked ourselves into believing that this missing piece is something mysterious and difficult to attain, but really it is the most natural thing in the world.

The desire to return to center and remember who we are is extremely strong; we feel an insatiable desire to search. And search we do. We look high and low; we look to family and friends, jobs, sex and drugs, and college degrees; we look for money, prestige and physical beauty. The ego allows us to search. In fact, the ego actively encourages us to seek. This searching is what defines the ego and is really its only line of defense against Self-realization. The ego's whole defense system is centered upon having us search for fulfillment where it can't be found. This temporarily satisfies our need to seek out home and simultaneously ensures we will not get there. And that is exactly why it is so important to cultivate a yoga or meditation practice that is not goal-oriented. Our spiritual practice is a time to retrain our minds to stop seeking for contentment in a new conquest or achievement. It's a time to pull the mind back from its constant searching and learn how to sit in the present moment. When we do this, we free the mind from the constant searching that causes us to forget our true identity as Atman.

Last week, one of my newer students, Jose, was in class. His practice was very new, but it was obvious that he was ready to dive head first into yoga. He was the son of Mexican immigrants who had come to the United States to make a better life for themselves and their children. Jose was about four years old when he came to the States. Because he was quite poor growing up, he had vowed to become wealthy. He studied hard in both high school and college, and landed a great job in a San Francisco advertising agency. By the time he was thirty, he was earning a very sizable salary and had the proverbial corner office. Jose had achieved what his parents had always hoped for, and was living the standard American dream.

All was not well, however. His body was always in pain, and he suffered from migraine headaches. His fiancée had left him because he spent far more time at work than he did with her. He was miserable. His doctor couldn't find anything wrong and recommended that he try yoga. Yoga worked like a charm. His headaches went away almost overnight and the tight knots in his back, neck and shoulders began to loosen.

During one class, however, something else began to let go. As I led the class into a final meditation, I couldn't help but notice his smile. It was so bright I had to smile myself. After class I asked him how he was doing, and he gave me a big hug. "I haven't felt like I did during this class since I was a little boy," he said. "For as long as I can remember, I have been rushing from one thing to the next. I guess I always thought that I would find peace when I had more money, but the more money I have made, the less happy I have become. When I was poor and living with my parents, I was at peace. Until I found yoga, I couldn't sleep at night from the stress. This yoga stuff is amazing."

According to the sacred texts, Jose is not alone. The constant searching for that peg that will fill the perceived hole in our being causes our pain. This is our core problem and the cause of all our suffering. It's not the food, money, sex or power that makes us unhappy—nor will the denial of these things ease our suffering only the recognition of our wholeness can make us feel whole.

About a year ago I was sitting on the beach feeling quite tranquil. When it came time to go, I gathered my things and put them in my backpack. I then realized that I could not find my sunglasses. I unpacked my bag several times, dug through the sand, and considered accusing the man next to me of stealing them. All the peace I had cultivated while on the beach that day was gone by the time I realized they were sitting on top of my head.

This is very reminiscent of our spiritual quest. We keep trying to find what we think we have lost, all the time losing our peace of mind and our sanity as we search. Ultimately, what we were looking for was never lost at all.

This searching is the bitter and ironic twist in the biography of our lives. We spend our lives looking and searching in every conceivable corner of the world for that one thing (or group of things) that will bring us the fulfillment we desire above all else, only to find that it is glowing deep within. It's the very act of searching that makes us lose ourselves. It's the very belief in deprivation that makes us feel deprived. It's the very act of trying to succeed that guarantees our failure, because even when we do get what we think we want, we realize we are still unhappy, and the search begins all over again. When we stand in the center of joy, searching for joy means seeking elsewhere, which then makes our lives feel joyless.

In other words, when we stop our searching and quiet our mind, we will feel complete. It's the search itself that makes us feel lost and incomplete. When we step onto the yoga mat or sit on the meditation cushion, we suspend that search and begin to realize how pointless it was in the first place.

"There is no fetter like illusion, no force greater than yoga,
no friend greater than knowledge and
no enemy greater than ego."
—GHERANDA SAMHITA 1:4

CHAPTER TWO

The Illusion of Maya

"Just as from studying the alphabet one may understand the scriptural teachings, so by practicing yoga, one may obtain knowledge of the Ultimate Reality."

—GHERANDA SAMHITA 1:5

MAYA: ILLUSION

"Conscious spirit and unconscious matter both have existed since the dawn of time, with maya appearing to connect them, misrepresenting joy as outside us."

—SHVETASHVATRA UPANISHAD I:9

When I began my practice I was astounded at its effect in my life. Not only was my body beginning to feel better, but also my heart was filled with compassion, and my mind was at peace more often than I had ever thought possible. However, there was one concept in yoga that made the hair on the back of my neck stand on end: that was maya.

Maya is the idea that our entire physical universe is an illusion—a figment of our collective and individual imaginations. According to sacred texts, the belief that the physical is real denies us the ability to experience our greatest potential. When I first heard this, I laughed. It seemed so absurd. It seems so evident that the physical universe is real; one can touch it and see it and smell it; it can be measured and studied and observed. Yet the great yoga masters have been very clear on this point and have held the concept of maya to be one of their greatest truths. The world of form and change is nothing more than an illusion—a fantasy of our collective imagination—a veil that has been placed before our eyes to allow each of us to keep up the illusions of our individual egos.

While the sages of India may have been among the first to realize the illusion of maya that is our physical universe, many since then have identified this same illusion. To a certain extent even modern physics has begun to identify maya. Albert Einstein,the father of modern physics, and in my opinion one of the great mystics of our modern era, said,

A human being is part of the whole called by us a universe—a part limited in time and space. He experiences himself, his thoughts and his feelings as something separate from the rest, a kind of optical delusion of his consciousness.

This delusion is a kind of prison for us; it restricts us to our personal decision and our affections to a few persons nearest to us. Our task must be to free ourselves from this prison by widening our circle of compassion to embrace all living creatures and the whole of nature in its beauty.

It's important that we look at maya squarely, for we will never feel freedom until we start to remove this veil from our eyes. Believing in maya is the cause of all suffering, because it perpetuates the belief in separation that fuels our egos and keeps us in bondage.

Maya is the spiritual equivalent of a pyramid scam that saps our resources and prevents us from making wise investments with our spiritual 'capital'. Until we withdraw our investments in maya, we will never be able to find the peace we so deeply desire; to invest in maya is to believe that we are small.

Maya is another one of those basic principles that make up the foundation of yoga. As long as we believe maya to be our ultimate reality, we are going to suffer. The reason for this is profoundly simple: everything in maya changes. Change is the characteristic that defines maya, so all things within it must take form and then pass back to dust, only to take a new form. Mountains will become valleys, and oceans will become deserts. It is the nature of maya.

Maya is made up of our individual and collective judgments. In a sense it is like a computer-generated virtual reality. The computer uses a series of ones and zeros to create the illusion. Our minds use positive and negative judgments to construct the world we see outside. Yoga helps us to pierce through the illusion of maya by helping us to see the formlessness that lies behind the illusion. It is this illusion that makes up our time and space reality. Things seem to be solid and real. There are laws that seem to govern this reality, such as gravity, relativity, or thermodynamics, and it all seems to make so much sense—at least from where we stand. But when you really look at our physical reality from a spiritual point of view, there are a great number of things that just don't add up.

In the early years, as I began to explore my yoga practice more fully, I would go to hear great masters speak. I would read and consume books on yoga. I loved the practice and the philosophy, but I could feel anger coursing through me each time the subject of maya came up. It rocked the very foundation on which my whole world was built.

At that time I was also exploring some of the earth-based spiritualities, such as Wicca and Native American Spirituality. These systems seemed both to maintain the reality of the physical universe, as well as see the Earth and nature as a direct means through which to realize spiritual truth. It seemed I would be unable to reconcile these two parts of my spiritual life. I did my best to ignore the concept of maya altogether, and when it did come up, I would tune it out or channel my anger and frustration into the least destructive outlet I could find.

This went on for several years, until I found myself on retreat at the Kripalu Center. During one of the workshops we were exploring the second stage of Kripalu yoga. This style of yoga is characterized by holding various poses for long periods. It is quite intense and frequently results in a deep emotional release. One of the exercises we did involved holding vrikshasana, the tree pose. We were led out of the main building and down a green grassy slope to a sizable pine grove. We were instructed to find a tree to face and then assume the tree pose. We were to hold each side until we heard a chime. Five minutes went by, and still no chime. My legs and arms began to shake and tremble. Another few minutes went by and my mental judgment rose to a fever pitch. Finally the chime rang and I was able to switch sides. At times I thought I might cry or laugh, but I stuck it out. I kept trying to quiet my mind and surrender into the pose.

All at once, my mind seemed to stop. I noticed the tree in front of me in a new way. It was pulsing with energy. The colors were brilliant. I felt as if I was seeing a tree for the first time. I smiled and allowed myself to sink deeper. The pain and challenge of the pose was somewhere in the background. As I went deeper and deeper into the pose, the tree began to change form. It seemed to melt into its surroundings. There was no distinction between the tree and the grove or between the tree and the earth that sustained it. Then I felt my body changing and becoming one with the tree. I could feel my roots reaching deep into the earth, and my branches reaching high toward the sun. Being a tree felt every bit as natural as being a human. I was the same but my form had changed. The whole physical universe became fluid, and time and space lost all meaning for me. I knew in that moment that the tree was Spirit masquerading as a tree, and I was Spirit disguised as a human. I knew for the first time that there was only One that took shape in the many.

As I heard the chime, I knew I needed to come back, but I didn't want to. In those last few breaths I understood maya. I fell to the ground in child pose and could feel the pulse of the earth. I was no longer conflicted by my earth-based spirituality or even my worldview. Maya actually validated these beliefs and enhanced my experience in this physical world.

What happened to me was a brief glimpse of what lies behind the veil of maya. Our egos have us convinced that we are physical and that our physical experience is what defines us. This couldn't be more wrong. I am no more a human body than that tree, which seemed so solid, was really a tree. Spirit exists within all things, and takes many forms on the canvas of maya. Sometimes Spirit takes the form of a tree or a rock or a planet— other times as a human or an animal. It's as if God is playing hide-andseek with Herself; when we peek behind the veil of maya, we see that beautiful divine light hiding there. Once we do this, we can enjoy the world with new eyes. We can detach from the physical and really begin to enjoy it. The physical universe is like a great piece of artwork created by Spirit. When we confuse it with something it is not, it becomes the weapon of the ego. The Mona Lisa is a great piece of art, but you would view it as a weapon if you were hit over the head with it. Likewise, understanding maya doesn't make the physical a bad thing. It allows us to step back and appreciate its beauty without having it blind us to our true nature as the eternal Atman.

———————— **LILA: THE DIVINE PLAY** ————————

"He resides in the city with nine gates which is the body. He moves in the world enjoying the play of his countless forms. He is the master of the universe, of animate and inanimate."
—SHVETASHVATARA UPANISHAD 3:18

This illusion we live in is not bad per se. It's only a problem when we confuse it with our ultimate reality. It can be used quite effectively for our joy, our entertainment and our learning, but it is not real and can never be made real. Learning to use the illusion to our advantage is very important; otherwise the ego will use its smoke and mirrors to delude the seeker further. In yoga there is a concept called lila or "The Divine Play." Traditionally this play was seen as a dance between the Hindu god Shiva and his consort Shakti, but I find it helpful to view it in more human terms. By understanding this concept we can create more fulfilling lives here in the physical universe, while at the same time moving closer and closer to Self-realization.

When I was in high school, one of my English teachers, Mrs. Nardone, took a group of students to see a play on Broadway in New York City. I wasn't all that interested in the play, but it was an opportunity to get out of school for the day. In my mind it might as well have been a field trip to a minefield in some war-torn country—it didn't take much to step out of my daily high school drudgery. What was surprising to me was that I really enjoyed the play. The sets were spectacular, and the actors were so believable that I found myself getting lost in the experience. I laughed out loud a few times, and at other times I subtly brushed back tears. (Nothing would have been more damaging to my sixteen-year-old male ego than getting caught with tears in my eyes.)

This experience was different than watching a movie or a TV show. I was right there with the characters. The actors were alive and I could see them having all the emotions their characters were having. I couldn't believe how fast the time went by. It was as if I had been transported into another world...and then all of a sudden, we were giving the actors a standing ovation.

Lila is the cosmic version of a Broadway play. The only difference is that in this play we are the actors. Lila is like a great epic in that it has many facets; there are phases of great light and happiness, and there are phases of darkness and despair. From where each of us stands on the stage, it is hard to comprehend the overall plot or story arc because we only have our own small role to play. But when we look back on history, we can see how the story of life in the physical universe has had purpose and how there seems to be the greatest drama unfolding around us. By exploring this divine play, we can gain great insight into our roles in the universe and our overall spiritual quests.

Stepping up to our role on the stage of life is not easy. Just as Arjuna sat on the battlefield of life, filled with despair and wanting to quit, it can be easy for each of us to look at the events of the world and to get depressed. But stepping into our roles in this divine play is an essential part of waking up to our true nature—Atman.

THE STAGE

It's on the stage of maya that lila is acted out. As we have already noted, the physical universe is an illusion. In many ways it's like a stage or Hollywood set. It is devoid of meaning until the actors bring the stage to life. Even though it is hollow and meaningless in and of itself, it is this stage that creates the backdrop against which the actors can present the story.

Many well-meaning spiritual seekers have tried to deny the physical and declare it unreal or evil. I feel this is unwise, because for most of us the physical seems to be very real. Calling it names is not going to make it seem less real to our ego perceptions; in fact, it could make it seem even more solid and tangible.

There is a story of a great meditation master. A man came to him and asked for the quickest path to enlightenment. The man didn't want to toil with years of spiritual practice or the distractions of the world and said he would do anything to attain instant enlightenment. The master confided in him that there was a way, but that no one had yet been able to do it. The man insisted that he at least be allowed to try. The wise old master agreed and told him to light a candle and walk into every room in the large ashram and repeat the sacred Gayatri Mantra (The Rig Veda 3:62) The master assured him that by the time he reached the last room, he would be enlightened.

The man was overjoyed. This seemed like a simple enough task. So he picked up a candle, lit it and began his walk toward the first room. Just as he was taking his first step, the master tapped him on the shoulder and said, "One more thing—while you are doing this, you must not think about the white mouse." The man had no idea what the master meant by this odd statement, and he proceeded. He didn't get past the second room before his mind began wondering what the master meant by 'white mouse.' He wondered whether he would encounter it while he was doing this sure-fire practice. By the time he got to the fifth room, he was consumed by the idea of this white mouse and left the master in search of an easier path.

Trying to deny the physical universe is like trying not to think about the white mouse. The more you try to push it out of your mind, the more power you give it. Therefore, embracing lila is a fundamental part of living as an urban mystic.

Denying the physical would be like going to a great play and complaining that the set doesn't look real enough. No matter how elaborate the set might be, it is still just a set. The goal in creating a good set is not to trick the audience or the actors into thinking that it is the real thing. It is there to enhance the overall experience and nothing more.

While it is not wise to constantly criticize the stage, it is also not wise to delude ourselves into believing that it is our ultimate reality. The physical universe is our stage, and on it we are called to give a command performance—only in the end, the actors go home, and the stage again is lifeless.

In fact, the hardest part about living in the urban world while keeping our spiritual focus may be this one idea, that we are called to be fully in the illusion without trying to find our innate value and worth there. The value of an actor is not found in the set; it is found in his or her ability to bring that set to life.

When you step onto the stage of lila, you have a choice. You can drag yourself across the stage like you have been mixing Quaaludes with alcohol, or you can step into the universal spotlight like a great diva. The stage is set; the roles have been cast. In experiencing the passion of lila, the first step is to take command of the stage that is your life and develop a stage presence that embraces the fullness and complexity of your role on the stage of maya.

THE ACTORS

In one sense this play has many actors and supporting actors, but in reality, there is only one—God. I often remind my students that we are all 'God in drag.' Remember, God is One, and as actors in the Divine play, we are God playing various roles. Just as the actors of a regular play are only playing roles and will let go of their characters when the play ends, so will it be with lila. When our roles are done we will return to the awareness of Atman within.

There are many roles we can play on the stage of lila. In fact, many of us are called to play multiple roles in this and other lives. This is where the concept of reincarnation fits in nicely. Even if you don't believe in reincarnation, it's easy to see how we can assume many roles in one lifetime. At times we can play a lead role and at other times we step to the side and become supporting actors.

Not all the roles are human either. Spirit can play the role of any life form or energy. In other words, Spirit does many forms of drag, and if we quiet our minds enough, we can see Spirit masquerading as plants and animals, planets and stars, etc. Anywhere there is change, growth and evolution, Spirit is dancing behind the veil of maya.

As actors in lila, we are called to play our human roles to the fullest. Perhaps our role is to work toward some social or environmental cause. Maybe we are called to raise a family or create art or literature. For most of us there will be a variety of aspects to our roles in this play. Whatever the calling, we will not be satisfied until we take center stage and own the spotlight.

When I was in college, my cousin approached me with a business opportunity. It was one of those multilevel marketing programs where the people at the top make a lot of money and the people at the bottom lose their shirts. I wasn't that excited about the products that were being sold, and I had no real drive to go out and make this thing work. The only thing that motivated me was the idea of making a quick buck. I lasted for about six weeks before I decided to get out altogether. I was very unhappy and each day that I tried to sell the stuff or to sign up someone else, I felt like I was selling a piece of my soul. When I finally decided to let it all go, I made a promise to myself that I would never again do anything that I did not feel a deep desire to do. I never wanted to work 'for the money' again. I wanted to have a purpose in my life, and I knew I would not find it in a job I hated or a relationship that wasn't heart-felt.

Being an actor in lila means following the script of your heart. Each of us has a very important role to play. We each have a purpose and a function here. When we learn to read from our own Spiritual script, we become divas on the stage of life. When we try to read from someone else's script, we get beaten and battered by the ego. We forget who we are, and depression and ill health become inevitable.

THE COSTUMES

Like a traditional play, the actors on the stage of lila have costumes. For human beings, these costumes take the form of bodies. Some bodies are healthy; others are sickly. Some bodies have dark skin, while others have light skin. In this play our bodies are the chief way in which Spirit disguises Herself. When we take on our body costumes, they are sometimes beautiful and sometimes ugly. Sometime they are torn and tattered, and sometimes they sparkle with rhinestones and sequins. Our costumes are very important to our roles, but they do not define who we are.

One year my mother took my brother, sister and me to see Phantom of the Opera in New York City. The playbill had photos of all the actors. On the ride home I was looking through the playbill and was struck by how handsome the actor who had played the Phantom was in real life. Of course, he didn't look quite so charming on the stage. When he was in his role as the Phantom, his face was completely disfigured. It was hard to believe he was the same person. The contrast between the actor's good looks and the Phantom's disfigurements was amazing.

It is important to wear our costumes well, without confusing them with the actors. Many times we go through life confusing our own and others' physical strengths and weaknesses with the real thing, rather than seeing behind the costumes to the handsome actors within. I work a lot with HIV positive people, and the one thing I like to stress is the importance of how a person relates to the virus. Many people will say things like, "I'm HIV," which is very unfortunate. HIV and a weakened immune system may be part of the body costume, but it is not who we are. As yogis we seek to wear our costumes proudly, while never forgetting who we are underneath the circumstances of our bodies.

There is an affirmation in the yogic tradition that states:
I am not my body.
I am not my thoughts.
I am not my emotions.
I am the witness and the observer.

This is a strong reminder of how we should perform our role in the cosmic play—acknowledging the body, mind and heart, but never confusing them with our own identity as a spark of the divine.

CHAPTER THREE

Kundalini
and the Flow of Life

*"The world is the river of God,
flowing from him and flowing back to him."*
—SHVETASHVATARA UPANISHAD 1:5

PRANA AND THE SUBTLE BODY

*"Prana is born of the Self. As a man casts a shadow,
the Self cast prana into the body at the time of birth so that
the mind's desires may be fulfilled."*
—PRASHNA UPANISHAD 3:3

One of the great confusions people encounter in the practice of yoga has to do with the body. There seems to be an innate contradiction between yogic philosophy and yogic practice. For most of us, we begin our yoga practice on the yoga mat with poses and breathing. We focus on the body by working to open it and become more comfortable with being in the physical. But a simple scan of the Yoga Sutra or the Bhagavad Gita will cast the body in a very dim light. Even the most liberal yogis see the body as an illusion, and more conservative yogis see it as a heavy anchor tethering the soul to the painful world of form and suffering.

This seeming contradiction was very difficult for me. Being raised Roman Catholic, I was used to a lot of shame being placed on the body. Everything from diet to sexuality was subtly or overtly put down. Finding hatha yoga was such a welcome relief from that shame; I began to learn a deep love and respect for my body, which helped me to heal in so many ways.

Section Two of this book deals with the eight limbs of yoga which are also called raja or royal yoga. Hatha yoga, which is the most popular style of yoga in the West, is deeply rooted in raja yoga, but it is also deeply rooted in kundalini yoga. Kundalini yoga is the yoga of energy that moves through the body and gives it life.

Thus, hatha yoga, be it a gentle restorative practice or a more active flowing practice, is really the love child of two other styles of yoga, raja and kundalini. If you really want to understand hatha yoga, a basic knowledge of both traditions is essential. In this chapter, we will explore the energetic (kundalini) aspect of yoga.

I was none too happy to read, "The aversion to one's own body and avoidance of contact with others comes from bodily purification" in the Yoga Sutras (2:40). It seemed like such a step backwards, but in time I began to learn more about yoga, and then the depth and meaning of its statements about the body started to become clear. Yoga does not view the body as bad; it simply helps us to realize that we are not the body. The body is simply the expression of a deeper truth. When we choose to identify with the body alone, we settle for less, but when we use the body as a doorway, we begin to transcend its limits.

As I mentioned, the body is an expression of a deeper truth. For thousands of years yogis have known what modern physics is just now beginning to discover—the universe seems solid to us only because we perceive it that way. In reality, the universe is a big sea of energy or life force known as prana. Prana is not just a static energy. It is dynamic and ever changing. It takes form for a while, and then dissolves back into formlessness. In one moment it may be a bird, and in the next a brilliant star. It is ever-changing and ever-flowing. It's like the water of a great river, which bends and flows within the banks of consciousness. Just as banks of the river are what bring form to the formless, our consciousness is what gives form to the flow of prana in our bodies, hearts, and minds.

Prana is the stuff of life, and the state of our consciousness will dictate what our experience of that life is like. Prana is flowing through you right now, and it is being guided, for better or worse, by your consciousness. If your health, your relationships, your emotional state or any other part of your life are not where you want it to be, you have a choice. You can sit around and complain, making yourself a victim, or you can start to reshape the banks of your river.

Several years ago I was at a meditation retreat. The retreat involved many hours of meditation each day and was quite intense.

As I sat one day, I could feel the familiar dull ache in my back, hips and knees. It felt as if they would explode if I didn't stretch them out. I was just about ready to pick up my meditation cushion and walk home when something snapped. The sensations of my body were still there, but I started to feel a pulse of energy that moved through me.

As I explored this energy, I began to notice that it was more 'me' than my physical body. My aching muscles and joints continued to make noise in the background of my awareness, and the energy that flowed through me became more and more real. I also started to notice that there was no place where 'my' energy ended and the rest of the universe started. I started to feel oneness. It was then that I felt inspired to revisit my aching back. I realized that my aching back was nothing more than the resistance I held about sitting. It seemed to have a lot to do with a deeply held belief about wasting time. I could almost hear my father telling me that sitting around doing nothing was just a form of laziness. As his words echoed in my mind, I could feel the dull ache grow in intensity. As I realized this, the whole belief system I had had around 'doing nothing' drifted away and my back pain disappeared.

The physical body (anamayakosha) is largely the effect of the subtle body (pranamayakosha), which are molded and shaped by our conscious and unconscious thoughts. When I say that they are the effects of this subtle body, I mean that the physical body is the result of patterns of movement (or in the case of disease, a lack of movement) in the energy body. Our thoughts are what direct the flow of our life force, and thus create mental, physical and emotional health or disease.

On a practical level, yoga acknowledges that we are experiencing life through a physical body and that we experience thoughts and emotions. The yogic approach to living in this world is opposite to what most of us have been taught. The texts of India speak of prana or 'life force', which is the stuff that gives the physical, emotional and mental bodies shape and form. We have already spoken of the illusion of this world, but we have yet to look at exactly how this world, and more specifically how the body, springs forth.

Prana is life. It's the difference between a block of wood and a living tree—or the difference between a corpse and a living body. Without prana there would be no physical universe, for it is the foundation. The entire physical universe is nothing more than a system of judgments which we hold collectively and individually and which slows or halts the flow of prana and then creates patterns with it. When filtered through our perception, that prana seems to be a bone or a muscle or a pile of dirt. But when we move beyond perception, we can see all matter as prana in disguise.

THE ENERGY PATHWAYS

"External signs appear when the nadis are pure.
The body will definitely be lean and bright."
—HATHA YOGA PRADIPIKA 2:19

This life force is carried throughout our subtle body through tiny pathways known as nadis. There are said to be at least 72,000 of these pathways in the human body. While this is a staggering number, some systems of yoga claim there are many more. Whatever the number, these tiny conduits bring life force to all parts of the subtle body. When these nadis get blocked with mental impurities and unexpressed emotions, the prana is not allowed to flow. Because our natural states of health and wholeness are dependent on a continuous flow of prana, blocks in our nadis create dysfunction in the body.

The first time I went to a nudist camp, I was very self-conscious. It seemed odd to see so many people living their lives naked. They were playing volleyball, walking dogs and jogging. Somehow, I had let a friend talk me into going, and at first I thought I had made the biggest mistake of my life. As luck would have it, I bumped into someone I knew. It was my friend Jeff's mom. As if seeing your friend's mom naked were not socially awkward enough, she had had a double mastectomy. There were two large scars where her breasts used to be. And still she sat there as if nothing was wrong.

Because she was reading and didn't see me, I decided to avoid her. I started to quietly back away, but just when I thought I was safe, she spotted me. She called my name and waved for me to come over.

There was no escaping, so I took a deep breath and walked over to her. I was careful to keep eye contact with her at all times so as not to look at her scars and offend her. I'm sure my discomfort was very evident. We had only talked for a few minutes, but already it felt like an eternity. I don't think I have ever been in such an awkward position. Seeing my angst, she smiled, took my hand and said, "Darren, it's okay to look. I am not embarrassed any more."

She then took my hand and placed it on her chest. I thought I would die. But because she made it okay, I started to relax. And I was able to be honest with myself and with her. I was no longer afraid of offending her because it was clear that she was very comfortable with herself. In that moment I was able to challenge my long-held beliefs about women's breasts, cancer, and a whole bunch of other things.

We had a great conversation that afternoon, and she went on to tell me something that I would later learn was a very yogic idea. "Darren, I spent my life being ashamed of my body. I hated my breasts because I was taught to think they were dirty. I didn't even breast feed my children because I felt it was unnatural. Imagine that, the most natural thing on earth, and I had let society tell me it was wrong. After I got cancer and had my surgery, I needed some serious psychotherapy. Through my counseling, I came to believe that my whole attitude toward my breasts is what had caused my cancer, or at least greatly contributed to it. After a lot of work, and a fair amount of courage, I decided to start coming to this camp. I want to feel good about my body, and I don't ever want to be ashamed of any part of who I am, because I know that if I keep things bottled up or deny a part of myself, it will make me sick again."

The release of old ideas and judgments that she referred to is how we clear these pathways, the nadis. When we practice yoga we are seeking to clear these pathways so that the energy can flow more freely and health and balance can be restored to the body. The experience of cleansing the nadis is called nadi shuddhi. Every unresolved emotion and psychological block, whether conscious or unconscious, gets held in our nadis. If we don't clear those blocks, dysfunction is sure to develop in the body.

One way of clearing these blockages in our energy body is by practicing hatha yoga. Each pose is designed to open up these channels of energy, and the breath helps us to flood the body with prana and direct that prana to the areas where we're working. The blockages held there are thus brought to our conscious awareness and we can then let them go.

This is why people have that great glow after a yoga practice. In a well-balanced yoga practice, all of the energy pathways get opened and cleared. This nadi shuddhi glow is one of the great gifts of yoga practice, and it is one of the first things that people notice early on. It feels as if every cell in the body is alive and pulsing with life. When we practice yoga consistently, we begin to work deeper and deeper into the nadis, and the deeper held blocks start to let go. This is what gives long time yogis that peaceful aura that even the casual observer notices.

When we clear these nadis, we reduce the chances of small problems occurring such as colds and fatigue, and we also reduce the chances of things like cancer and heart disease. This is not to say that there aren't external factors that affect our health, but our body's ability to cope with those factors is greatly increased when we keep the energy flowing.

Perhaps Jeff's mom would have developed cancer even if she hadn't held a lot of judgments about her breasts. Maybe she could have avoided the experience. Whatever the case, she is more open now, and her health— both mental and physical—has never been better. This is the result of letting go of old patterns and letting life flow freely through her.

Each time we come to the yoga mat, we surrender into the flow of life and we gradually begin to realize that health and wholeness are not things we acquire, but rather things we surrender into.

THE SEVEN CHAKRAS

"When the nadis are disrupted by impurities, the breath doesn't enter the middle. How can umani exist? How can the goal be attained?"
—HATHA YOGA PRADIPIKA 2:4

As I mentioned, there are at least 72,000 nadis in the human body. While it is not important to know all of them, it is helpful to know a few of the major pathways, as they have a very direct impact on how and why we practice yoga.

The main channel of energy in the body is called the sushumna and it runs directly through the spine. Many nadis flow out of the sushumna and travel out to the rest of the subtle body. This is why so much focus in hatha yoga is placed on the spine. If this channel of energy is blocked or shut down, all the other nadis are affected. Once we open this channel of energy, a major step has been taken.

In addition to the sushumna, there are two other nadis that are quite important. They are the ida and the pingala. These two nadis work closely with the sushumna. Both start at the base of the spine and then wrap around the sushumna like two vines growing up a tree. The ida and the pingala are responsible for balancing the two sides of the brain and consequently, the two sides of the body.

The ida and the pingala originate at the base of the spine (in the first chakra) and cross each other at four points along the sushumna. They climb as high as the forehead where they end in the sixth chakra. Some texts place the first six chakras between these intersections while others place the major energy centers over each intersection. A seventh chakra is found at the top of the head and some texts refer to additional chakras above that.

A chakra is a vortex of energy in the subtle body. Chakras are frequently described as spinning wheels of energy. There are quite a few throughout the body, but the seven major chakras along the spine are of the greatest concern to the modern yogi.

People who are able to see auras can frequently see the seven chakras and can determine a person's relative health on physical, mental and emotional levels by noticing how they spin and how congested they are. In her book Hands of Light, Barbara Ann Brennan, describes chakras as "two funnels that are placed end to end with the sushumna running between them, each of them spinning and exchanging information with the outside world. I like to think of them like little whirlpools in a stream."

While it may be helpful to be able to visualize the seven chakras, it is of far greater importance to understand their significance in our spiritual practice. I think of each of the chakras like a compact disc— they contain programmed information that is recorded and played back. This information can be recorded or erased, or played on a repeat cycle as often as the mind allows. When we practice yoga, we bring our awareness to these chakras, whether consciously or unconsciously. As we become more aware of this programming, we can make more conscious choices about it. We can keep the programming, erase it or replace it. This programming can take the forms of tightness in the physical body, repressed emotions or rigid thought paradigms. Each of the yoga poses works to open and balance one or more chakras. When we do this, blocks in those chakras get released and our programming in the respective chakra gets healed.

Each of the seven major chakras is responsible for a different aspect of our being. In order to be self-actualized, we need to have all the chakras working in concert with one another and relatively free from blocks. Most of us have glimpses of this balance from time to time, but very often we get stuck in one chakra or another and try to get it to function for all the others. This creates a great imbalance in our bodies, hearts and minds, which is frequently reflected in the external circumstances of our lives.

In order to understand how the yoga practice affects these energy centers in the body, let's turn our attention to each of the seven major chakras and explore their role in our yoga practice.

Muladhara

The first chakra, muladhara, is physically located at the base of the spine. This is the seat of physical survival. It is where we learn how to feed and clothe ourselves, and how to live and function in the context of a society or tribe. When this chakra is out of balance we frequently experience lower gastro-intestinal problems and/or tightness in the legs and feet. Mentally we tend to be flaky or ungrounded, and things in the physical world are perceived to be difficult. When we balance this chakra in our yoga practice, many of these physical conditions are replaced with health and wholeness. Both our external and internal lives seem to become more organized and purposeful, and life seems more abundant.

It's important to note that a person's external circumstances are not a good indicator of the condition of the first chakra. A better indicator is the reaction to those circumstances. For example, there are very wealthy people who live their lives from a mindset of complete scarcity, even though they want for nothing. Likewise, there are people who feel a deep sense of abundance and yet have very little in the way of material things.

Svadhisthana

The second chakra, svadhisthana, is located between the pubic bone and the navel. It's the seat of our sexual and creative energies. It's here that we feel the desire (or lack of desire) to procreate. It's also where our sexual orientation is defined and where we make decisions about romantic partnership. While the first chakra dictates how we interact with our society, this chakra determines how we interact with a partner or partners.

Physical symptoms that can indicate an imbalance in this chakra include prostate, uterine, testicular, ovarian and vaginal problems such as cancer, inflammation, sexual dysfunction, and recurring infections. Bladder and urinary tract infections are also common. Tightness in the hips, buttocks and lower back can also indicate some blocked energy.

In addition to procreation, it is the seat of creative energies. It's here that we move beyond the first chakra's survival-based preoccupations to our vocation or life's work. When the first and second chakras are not in balance with each other, we find one of two extremes—the workaholic or the starving artist. By balancing the second chakra, we heal conflicts around our sexuality and break unhealthy patterns in our romantic relationships. We also let our creative juices flow, and we begin to become more balanced in our relationships with our parents and/or our children.

Manipura

The third chakra, manipura, is the seat of one's identity and personal power. Its physical location is just above the navel. When this chakra is in balance, we experience a healthy sense of Self. The Self is defined outside of ego terms such as age, race, sexual orientation, gender and occupation. The statement, "I am," doesn't need to be followed by an external condition or description to be meaningful.

To the degree that manipura is out of balance and blocked, however, the ego will run the show that is our life. On a physical level, an imbalance in this chakra usually manifests in the abdominal organs. Conditions such as ulcers, digestive problems, and blood sugar issues are more likely.

Manipura is also the emotional center of the body. While the other chakras also process emotions, this chakra is where we tend to hide unwanted emotions and experience base emotions. Thus we can experience 'gut feelings' or a feel a 'pit in the stomach'.

Anahata

Anahata is the fourth chakra and is located between the shoulder blades and over the breastbone. It's often referred to as the heart chakra, and it is here that we experience love, compassion, forgiveness and mercy. When this chakra is fully open, love fills us and pours out to others.

All forms of love—romantic love, parental love, friendship, and ultimately a love for all beings—are experienced here. When this chakra is fully open we are able to know God in all beings. People like Mother Theresa displayed a heart center that was very open.

When this chakra is out of balance or blocked, jealousy, bitterness, fear, resentment and hardness take the place of love. The heart chakra also controls the cardiovascular system and the thymus gland, which is responsible for healthy immune functioning. Therefore, when there is a blockage in anahata, it can result in heart disease, high blood pressure and a weakened immune system.

Visshudha

At the throat area we find visshudha, the fifth chakra. This energy center is the seat of communication and communion. It's in this area that we find the need to understand and be understood. This is where we share ideas, both good and bad, and develop means of communication that can range from rudimentary language skills to the written word.

When this chakra is out of balance or blocked, we use our ability to communicate in ways that hurt rather than heal. Rather than insight, we inspire ignorance. Collectively, we try to shout above others rather than use our voices in concert with one another. On a physical level, weaknesses in this chakra often manifest as sore throats and infections in the throat and lungs. Thyroid and metabolism problems are also common, as are frequent bouts of laryngitis.

When this chakra is open and balanced, communication becomes more fluid. Our internal dialog becomes more honest and in accord with our true nature as Atman. The words we speak to others are clear, direct and honest, as are other forms of communication. We also become comfortable with silence and use our words to convey meaningful ideas rather than to fill empty spaces.

Ajna

The sixth chakra, ajna, is located at the point between the eyebrows. It is the center of perception and cognition. On a physical level it regulates the lower brain functions and the five physical senses. It also helps us to interpret the information that these senses bring to us from our perceived external world.

On a spiritual level, this is the center responsible for the so-called 'sixth sense.' It's here that we find things like intuition, visions, and mystical experiences. We all have, to a greater or lesser degree, a veil in front of this chakra; this veil is known as perception. This perception filters what gets taken in and warps it to fit the picture of reality that our ego seeks to uphold. A person's spiritual practice seeks to remove this veil so that we can see things as they are, rather than how the ego would have us perceive them.

Imbalances in ajna can manifest in mental illness, such as schizophrenia, headaches, brain tumors and seizures. In past cultures, people with imbalances in this area have been labeled 'demon possessed.' Today they are labeled 'mentally ill.' Whatever the organic cause of a person's mental illness, meditation and yoga have proven to be quite effective in helping people with a variety of conditions to find mental health and balance.

Sahasrara

The seventh chakra is located at the crown of the head and is our connection to Spirit. Its Sanskrit name is sahasrara. While the muladhara roots us and grounds us in our physical nature, sahasrara roots us in our spiritual nature. It's here that we strive and reach for the heavens, and where we find a deep yearning to evolve and realize our true nature as Atman.

When this chakra is out of balance, we frequently have blocks around our spiritual life. These blocks can manifest in either of two extremes. On one end is the religious zealot whose hard and fast dogmas prevent him or her from really knowing Spirit at all. On the other end are the spiritual denialists who won't even acknowledge they have a spiritual nature.

When we open this center, we allow a direct revelation. Rather than experience God in the context of myth or religious dogma, we literally KNOW. This experience is called samadhi and will be covered in great detail in Chapter Twelve.

—— THE CHAKRAS AS A SYSTEM ——

It's easy to see these chakras as completely separate, having little to do with each other, and to pick and choose favorites, but this is very dangerous. The seven major chakras each contribute to the whole experience of being human. When we let one get out of balance or shut down, we process life in unbalanced ways and we fill the chakras with conflicting programs.

When I was in college, I worked for a suicide hotline. On one of the all-night shifts I received a call from a woman who was very distressed. She had taken several handfuls of sleeping pills and was drinking as well. Her intention, of course, was to end her life.

As we talked, she told me that she had just had an abortion and felt very guilty about it. She was raised in a very religious home, and she knew her parents would never forgive her. In fact, her parents' beliefs about abortion were so influential that she had considered having the baby. Her friends, however, had some very different beliefs. They felt she was too young and too immature and pressured her to abort the pregnancy. This created a great conflict in the tribal aspect of her first chakra. Because she had so many radically different beliefs held in this center, either decision would have led to a deep split in that part of her mind.

Her second chakra was also in conflict. She told me she had been afraid to tell her boyfriend that she was pregnant, because she didn't know if he would want her to keep the child or abort. She wasn't even sure if he would stay with her. In addition, her feelings about parenting came into play. On the one hand she was unprepared to raise a child, but on the other hand she felt like abortion was murder. This of course left her with even more conflict.

Her ultimate decision to abort hit her much harder than she had expected, and she had decided to end her life. Unfortunately, the most I could offer her that night was a sympathetic ear. She declined all my offers to call for help, and eventually went unconscious while we were on the phone.

This is, of course, an extreme case. Most of us don't experience that degree of conflict within our chakras, but for most of us there can be a considerable amount. Look, for example, at how easy it is to confuse the roles of the second chakra's sexual needs and desires with the heart's need for love and intimacy.

In theory, the chakras should all work together, but when we fill them with conflicting beliefs, judgments and unprocessed emotions, disease and imbalance occur at all levels of the body, heart and mind.

KUNDALINI

"Kindle the fire of kundalini deep in meditation.
Bring your mind and breath under control.
Drink deep of divine love,
and you will attain the unitive state."
—SHVETASHVATARA UPANISHAD

Understanding each of the seven chakras as individual energy centers is quite helpful in allowing us to balance the various aspects of our health and humanity. But their place in our spiritual evolution is also important. In order to understand this, we need to explore the concept of kundalini-shakti.

In Chapter Two we discussed the idea of Lila. This Divine Play is acted out by Shiva and his lover Shakti. Within our bodies, this happens through the kundalini experience. Shiva and Shakti are the divine lovers who act out their romance on the cosmic stage. Within our bodies this cosmic dance is happening all the time. Shiva exists in his formless state at the crown of the head in sahasrara. Shakti, his consort, exists as a large coil of energy called kundalini-shakti situated at the base of the spine wrapped around muladhara. Like two lovers filled with passion for each other, Shiva and Shakti yearn to unite and become one. Therefore, over and over again, Shakti seeks to reach her lover and experience union with him by traveling up the sushumna.

This kundalini-shakti energy is often depicted as a snake, and much of the time it lies fairly dormant. On occasion, this energy will stir and begin its journey up the spine, rising as high as we are capable of letting Her. In order for Her to ascend, each chakra needs to be free of blockages. Consequently, in our journey to Self-realization, it is essential that we open each of these energy centers so that Shiva and Shakti can be united within us.

Because She begins her journey at the root chakra and moves up the spine along a vertical axis, She must move up the spine through each chakra in succession. For example, if you have a very open third chakra, but your first and second chakras are blocked, the energy will only be able to flow as high as the lowest chakra that is open. It is for this reason that it is wise to clear out the lower chakras before attempting to work on the upper chakras. A lot of well-meaning spiritual seekers want to go for the gusto and experience Spirit directly in their first few yoga classes.

I had a student named Scott, who came to me a few years back and asked me to recommend a book that would help him understand the spiritual part of yoga. I recommended Autobiography of a Yogi by Paramahansa Yogananda. In this book Yogananda recounts his life in great detail. He speaks of the great yogis he has met who have special powers, such as the ability to levitate or the ability to appear in two places at once.

At first glance, the book might seem to be a work of fiction, but there is good documentation of great yogis doing seemingly impossible things. In any case, Scott was quite impressed and asked me to help him learn to levitate. I had to laugh when he asked. Not only do I not know how to levitate myself, but it takes a very advanced yogi even to consider such things.

He seemed a bit disappointed, so I had him re-read the first few chapters of Yogananda's book. In the early years of his life, Yogananda wanted nothing more than to run off and find his guru, live in a hermitage and meditate for hours each day. His father wouldn't hear of it, so Yogananda ran away several times. Ultimately, he agreed to finish his schooling before formally renouncing the world to live as a monk.

Yogananda is one of the great yogis to come to this country from India, and he has had a great impact on yoga in the West. But even he needed to deal with the lower chakras before he could devote his life to the higher ones. As urban mystics, we need to be really clear about our relationship to our lower chakras, because we don't have the convenience of being able to let go of our worldly responsibilities.

Ultimately, it was Yogananda's ability to live and work in the world that enabled him to take his great spiritual insights and offer them to thousands of people everywhere. This is why the first job of a good yoga teacher is to get a new student back in touch with his or her body. Until we really ground ourselves in the root chakra, it will be difficult, if not impossible, to excel as modern yogis. Once we clear out the root chakra, we are able to look more closely at the second chakra, and then the third, and so on. This is not to say that we shouldn't work on all the chakras all the time. Indeed, a well-balanced yoga practice should work to open all the energy centers. But the general focus of our spiritual evolution should be to start working through the bottom chakras first, working our way up the spine. In other words, today we balance the checkbook; tomorrow we levitate.

THE GIFT OF THE GURU

"He runs without feet and holds without hands.
He sees without eyes and hears without ears.
He knows everyone, but no one knows him.
He is called the First, the Great, the Supreme."
—SHVETASHVATARA UPANISHAD 3:19

This slow ascent up the sushumna may seem a work that will take lifetimes, and by all conventional measures it will. But when we find the willingness to grow faster, Spirit has a way of putting us on the fast track.

While yoga is one of the fastest ways I have found to Self-realization, it is still a lot of work. The pile of baggage we become aware of when we come to the yoga mat can seem so large that it may appear there's no point in even trying.

This is where the guru comes in. Gurus have been given a bum rap over the past twenty or so years, and much of this criticism is justified. When I first started looking for my guru, I was convinced that tax evasion, expensive cars and inappropriate sexual contact with followers were part of the job. This, of course, is not the case, but with all the scandal over the past few years, one can see where people might be a little hesitant to trust someone who is called a guru.

The word guru means "darkness to light." Therefore, a true guru seeks to lead his or her student to light. Gurus can be very different in personality and approach, but before we can talk about gurus it is important to know where the legitimate ones get their authority. The Sadguru, or great teacher, is the universal teacher that is within all beings. This Sadguru is not unique to yoga. It has been called by many names, in many cultures. It is always present if we are able to listen. It is that small voice within you that knows exactly what you need in any moment. When we listen to this voice, blocks in our consciousness get removed—sometimes gently, sometime forcefully, but always for our greater good.

When we really surrender to this universal teacher, we can have moments of great revelation that change us forever. Oftentimes this revelation involves an awakening of the kundalini energy, which rushes up the spine and burns away impurities in all of the chakras impurities that could have taken lifetimes to work through. This experience is known as a kundalini awakening.

When we have a sexual orgasm, we generally feel it in the second chakra. If we are in a love-based, fourth chakra relationship, we can feel the orgasm as high up as the heart. When we have a kundalini experience, we have something like an orgasm but much more intense because it travels through all of our chakras. In fact, sexual arousal is the beginning of a kundalini experience—the only difference is that most often we only let the energy rise to the second chakra before we 'climax', so to speak. Most often, people having this kundalini experience will be moved to tears, or even to a seizure-like experience where they fall to the floor and shake violently. (I suspect that Christian 'holy rollers' have something like a kundalini awakening, though I doubt most of them would agree with me.)

Because this universal teacher is not physical, most of us are unable to surrender to her fully on a regular basis. She can easily seem quite removed from the trials of our day-to-day life. Therefore, it is unlikely that we will be able to trust her enough to allow our chakras to open and the kundalini to flow freely. It is for this reason that she sometimes works through human gurus. A guru is more than just a teacher. He or she helps us to open our chakras and nadis so that we can allow kundalini-shakti to move up our spine.

Generally, the guru has achieved a certain degree of spiritual mastery, but this is not always the case. Like the rest of us, gurus often wrestle with their human natures. Even the greatest gurus, from Buddha to Jesus, struggled with life; they fell from time to time and often experienced fear, grief and anger. Yet in spite of that, something came through them with which people were able to connect. It was through their humanity that the Sadguru was made so accessible to so many.

A guru's job is to bring the student from darkness to light. There are three main ways a guru can do this. Some gurus will do all three, while others will do just one or two. The first is called darshan. In darshan, the guru speaks or writes to his or her shishya or student and reveals truth through his or her words. If a guru is still in a body, this will frequently take the form of a sermon-like talk or discourse. If the guru has left his or her body, darshan is most often received by studying the teachings of that guru. A Western form of this idea can be seen when devout Christians study the Gospel or Jews study the Torah (Books of Moses).

A second way the guru can speed a student along the path is through sadhana. Sadhana means spiritual practice. Certainly you can develop your own spiritual practice by listening to the Sadguru within, but when working with a physical guru, spiritual practice is often given you like a prescription. The guru may have a standard set of techniques that he or she gives to all students or may customize the sadhana for each individual. In the case of hatha yoga certain poses may be given, or in the case of practices such as the Ashtanga Primary Series and Bikram Yoga, the founders offer a standard sequence of poses that are given to everyone.

The third way the guru can assist a student along the path is by shaktipat. When a guru gives shaktipat, the kundalini is awakened in the student. This can be done with a look or a touch, or even with a prayer. Sometimes the guru needs to be present in the room; at other times the guru can be in a distant location, or even deceased.

The gift of shaktipat can only be given to a student who is ready. It cannot be forced on anyone. It is a powerful and deeply moving experience that often leaves the recipient feeling spiritually renewed and uplifted. It can, however, be a bit unsettling if one is not expecting it.

The first time I went to hear Yogi Amrit Desai speak, I had no idea what shaktipat was. I was on retreat at the Kripalu Center, doing a work exchange. One of the guys in my group was from the South. His name was Jackson, and he spoke with a deep southern accent. He had a gruff, lumberjack-like appearance, with large hands and a little stubble on his face. In spite of his very masculine appearance and demeanor, he was a very openhearted and sensitive person.

We had become good friends, and decided to go hear the guru speak together. Neither of us had any idea what to expect. Everyone else seemed to be making a big deal out of it, so we decided to venture into this unknown together. When we got to the large room where the event was to take place, we immediately noticed that we were not appropriately dressed for the occasion. Everyone else was dressed in white. Some Indian style kirtan chanting had already begun, and people were dancing and moving wildly. Jackson and I sat down near the back of the room and felt awkward as we watched this spectacle. When the energy in the room had reached its pinnacle, a man at the front of the room blew into a conch shell. All at once everyone dropped to the floor with his or her head down. In walked the guru.

Both Jackson and I were sufficiently freaked out. I had visions of Jonestown dance through my head; I was just waiting for them to serve Kool-Aid! Yogi Desai took his seat at the front of the room and began to play his harmonium. He started to chant, and people chanted back in traditional Indian call and response. He didn't have the best voice, but there was something hollow and mystical about his tone—it was very hypnotic.

After a while he began chanting the sound of Om and people joined him in a beautiful and continuous chant. The whole room was alive and full of energy. Then I noticed that he was not chanting with the rest of us. He was making some slight jerking motions that resembled a hiccup. No sooner did I see this than people started to cry and shake. Some people were rocking violently as if in a rocking chair. Others were on the floor shaking. Still others were crying quietly.

I was in awe. I turned to look at Jackson in order to share this surreal moment with someone who was on the same page as myself, only to find he was on the floor sobbing, and in what appeared to be a mild seizure. Part of me wanted to call an ambulance, but he didn't seem to be in any danger. In fact, he seemed quite peaceful.

Eventually, things wound down. I was stunned. I didn't know what to say to Jackson. I wanted to know what it was like, and I wanted to know if he was okay. I could tell he felt awkward about having such an emotional episode so I let him calm down before giving him the twenty questions. Later that night we sat in the dining hall and chatted over tea. He recounted his experience in this way:

I really thought the whole thing was weird at first. You know, everyone dressed in white and dancing like drunken fools. We just don't do stuff like that back on the farm. I really didn't see what the big deal was until we started to chant Om. Then I could feel something stirring. Sorta like I was getting sexually aroused, but it wasn't sexual. It was like my whole body was tingling. Then I felt this weird sensation in my spine. It felt like a whole bunch of those big red fire ants crawling up the inside of my spine.

At first I was sort of scared, but then I relaxed, because it felt a lot like sex. You know—like you are getting really hot with someone, and the energy keeps building. I was starting to get into it, and then it really hit. It felt like I pissed on a spark plug or something. This bolt of energy that felt like electricity shot up my spine and my whole body fell to the floor.

I was so jolted that I had to cry. It wasn't a bad thing, and I wasn't sad. Actually I was more okay than I had ever been—it was awesome. I've never been one to get into God and all that kinda stuff, but this made me feel so small and larger than life all at the same time.

His words made me feel jealous. I wanted some of that experience for myself, but the timing was not right. As of this writing I have not experienced shaktipat from a guru, and who knows? I may never. I have had the opportunity to study a bit more, however. I have read accounts in other traditions that reflect this experience as well. For instance, the Bible is filled with examples of people being hurled to the Earth by the hand of God and having their lives changed in powerful ways.

The important thing to remember is that the gift comes from the Sadguru, not the guru. Finding a guru is not a prerequisite for spiritual growth, or even for a kundalini experience. Most gurus will tell you flat out that it is the Sadguru, not the guru him or herself, that graces us with an accelerated spiritual experience. Since that night with Jackson,

I have had the opportunity to speak with Yogi Desai. He insists that this shaktipat is not from him, but comes through him. Over and over again, he and other gurus (at least the legitimate ones) point to the inner Sadguru. They can only offer guidance and inspiration until we are ready to access that Sadguru directly. A real guru seeks to work him or herself out of a job by bringing the student to the light.

"Under the illumined teacher's guidance
they become united with the Lord of Love."
—TEJABINDU UPANISHAD 1:4

CHAPTER FOUR

Karma Yoga and Relationships as a Spiritual Practice

---

*"Selfish action imprisons the world.
Act selflessly, without any thought of personal profit."*
—BHAGAVAD GITA 3:9

THE NEW KARMA YOGA

*"The bodies of living beings are created by their good and bad
deeds; action is born of the body. Thus the [wheel] turns."*
—GHERANDA SAMHITA 1:6

Traditionally a yogi would renounce the world and live a cloistered and solitary life. Some yogis would live in a community setting such as an ashram or monastery. Others would live as hermits or take a vow of silence. Whatever the case, they were not socialites by any measure. This is perhaps the biggest difference between the mystics of years past and the newly emerging urban mystics of our times. We are living full-fledged social lives. We are still participating in human relationships that range from romance to casual acquaintances.

As urban mystics we have the challenging task of turning those relationships into a spiritual practice in and of themselves. For most people, the ego dominates the realm of relationships. We oftentimes relate to others out of fear, to fill an internal void, or to survive. These are all traits of the ego.

In order to use our relationships in a new way, we need to shift control over to the Sadguru or inner teacher so that our relationships are based on love, shared abundance and the desire to express our innate wholeness. In doing this we are able to turn every encounter with another being into a yoga pose of sorts, and relating to each other becomes as much a part of our spiritual practice as sitting to meditate.

THE EGO PROJECTION AND KARMA YOGA

"Strive constantly to serve the welfare of the world; by devotion to selfless work one attains the supreme goal of life. Do your work always with the welfare of others in mind."
—BHAGAVAD GITA 3:19

In Chapter One we explored the concept of the ego—the belief that an individual is small and finite. Because this concept is so totally insane and illogical, the ego needs to spend vast amounts of energy to keep us from looking at the obvious, and nowhere is this more evident than in the realm of human relationships.

All of our relationships, from the passing conversations with the cashier at the supermarket to the lifetime relationships we form with children, parents, friends, and romantic partners, have the potential of being based on ego or on Spirit. Karma yoga is the practice of stepping back and deciding to relate to any given person in a new way that is less ego-based and more spiritual. In doing this we are able to see the Truth in that person, while simultaneously seeing it in ourselves.

From the moment we meet people we start to tell a story about them and create an ego that we then project onto them. Sometimes their egos will agree with our ego projections. When this happens things run somewhat smoothly. At other times, the ego we project onto them will conflict with their own ego identity, in which case the relationship will experience strain and turmoil. In either case these egos we create for other people are not who they are. Atman exists within all beings, and when we project an ego onto an individual, we deny ourselves the ability to see that Light.

Often complete strangers will come up to me and ask if I'm an artist or a surfer because of my long hair. Without knowing anything about me, they assume things about me based on their past experience with men who have long hair. In fact, I am not an artist or a surfer—at least not in the traditional sense. These are fairly harmless stereotypes, and they certainly don't bother me. There are worse things to be called than an artist or a surfer, but is it is a very simple example of how we begin to tell a story about people without first getting to know them. This goes way beyond getting to know the facets of a person's life. The stories we tell about the people we 'know' well, such as family and friends, usually run much deeper and often are much harder to let go. This is why our parents can be among the hardest people to forgive.

The reason we project an ego onto everyone we meet is quite simple. In order for people to maintain the belief in their own egos, they need everyone else to be in agreement. This doesn't mean we have to agree on external things. Having a nemesis can be just as ego defining as having a friend. Look at the number of people in Israel who live as if being a Jew were defined by not being Arab, or vice versa. To our egos, it doesn't matter if we say, "I love you," or "I hate you," as long as we focus on the words and the stories, rather than quieting the mind long enough to see through that illusion to the spark of the divine within.

To practice karma yoga, we enter into service to our brothers and sisters. The form this service takes is irrelevant, as long as the intention behind that service is to give love rather than fill an ego need. This is an essential distinction because most of us enter into relationships with the desire to get. This can be true even if our intentions seem genuine and the other person or people benefit in some way from the generosity. In karma yoga, we seek to relate to people while seeing them for who they are—Atman. This can be a very difficult practice because it is so tempting to fall back into the old patterns of projection and making up stories. If we can refrain from this constant projection, we free ourselves and offer others an invitation to freedom as well.

One of the ways I feel drawn to practice karma yoga is by taking time to chat with homeless folks. In San Francisco, there is no shortage of people living on the street, and I have become friendly with several of the regulars on Castro Street. I will oftentimes pick up a few cups of coffee or tea and sit down on the side of the road to chat. It never fails to be a growth-filled experience.

On one occasion, I sat down with my friend Daniel. He looked a bit depressed, so I asked him what was going on. He told me that he was having a hard time being a good Christian, because several people that day had been unfriendly toward him. I asked him to explain how that made him less of a Christian.

"I've read the Bible, and it says that I am made in the image of God, but it is so hard to remember that when everyone just steps over you and treats you like dirt. When people do that, it is hard to love them because I forget that we are neighbors."

Although I thought I was sitting down to be nice to Daniel, it was Daniel giving me the gift that day. Karma yoga seems to be about helping other people, but is more like a cosmic Easter egg hunt in which Spirit has hidden pieces of wisdom and moments of clarity in places right in front of us. By taking the time to talk with Daniel that day, I was reminded of who I am and what I am called to be in this life. If I had not taken the time to sit with Daniel, I would have passed by a very special Easter egg.

When we practice karma yoga, we consciously try to dissolve the ego we are projecting and seek to uncover the Atman within. To do this we practice seva, or selfless service. There is no one right way to practice seva.

For one person it may mean working with the homeless; for another, it may be volunteering with children. There are countless areas of need in our world, and all of us are called to do our part. The need we seek to fill is not as important as filling it with love.

There is a Sufi story about a mystic who was walking down the street to a temple to pray and meditate. On his way there he passed the homeless, the infirm and the hungry. When he arrived at the temple and began to pray, he called out to God and asked, "Why have you not done something to ease all this suffering?" From the depth of his soul, a voice responded, "I did do something, I created you."

When we practice karma yoga, we become a part of the solution, rather than contributing to or ignoring the problem. Through our practice of seva, we realize that there is really only one problem—a lack of love based on a false identity. We also begin to understand that there is really only one solution, though it may take many forms. That solution is, of course, love.

Practicing karma yoga is much more than just doing nice things. It is a very honorable thing to feed the hungry or to work with the mentally ill, but it becomes a spiritual practice when it is done from a place of love and compassion. It is karma yoga only when we infuse action with compassion and clarity of perception.

Mother Teresa, one of the greatest karma yogis of modern time, was once asked if she ever got depressed by the fact that she would never succeed in healing all the lepers. Without a thought she replied, "I am not called to succeed, I am called to love."

At its highest expression karma yoga is not about acts of love, but rather about learning to love whoever is in front of you in the moment, regardless of their social status, behavior, words or actions. Like a hatha yoga practice, some poses will be harder than others. Learning to love small children may be easy for you, while learning to see Atman in the death row inmate may be much harder. In time, though, even the toughest poses can be mastered, and the most difficult ego projections can be withdrawn. It is this that allows us to experience the oneness of life.

THE YOGA OF
INTIMATE RELATIONSHIPS

"Every selfless act, Arjuna, is born from Brahman, the eternal, infinite Godhead. He is present in every act of service."
—BHAGAVAD GITA 3:15

It's one thing to make lofty statements such as, "We are all children of God." It's quite another thing to experience all people as children of God. For the longest time I found it easy to be loving and peaceful with complete strangers, but every time I had interactions with my father, I would leave angry. Keeping people at arm's length makes it easy to love, but taking the time to get to know someone well is where the real practice begins.

One day I was practicing yoga at home. I was having a nice practice and enjoying all the poses. Then it occurred to me that the reason I was enjoying the practice so much was because I was picking all the poses that came easily to me. While this practice felt great and certainly worked to open me up, it was not the most transformational practice because I had unconsciously avoided all the poses that were really difficult.

True transformation in a yoga practice comes from doing the poses we resist, while at the same time working to change the mind about the experience. Relationships are no different. It's easy to love the people who are nice to you, and it is certainly good to do that, but if we really want to grow, we need to look at the relationships that are difficult and strained. In these relationships we need to practice the principles of karma yoga with added attention, because it is here that real progress can be made.

Parents

For most of us our first relationship is with our parents. They are our first contact in this world, so it would be almost impossible not to have a relationship with them. Because our impressions of our parents start at birth, or perhaps earlier, it is likely that we will have vast misconceptions about them.

Of course, not everybody will have the same experience with his or her parents. Some people will experience very supportive parents who will make mistakes from time to time, but will convey an overall message of love and support. Others will be born to parents who are largely absent on some or all levels. Still others will be born to abusive situations.

Regardless of the way our parents acted and the messages that were given, as modern yogis we have only one primary function, and that is forgiveness. It's doubtful that we will escape childhood without placing a bunch of ego projections on our parents. Some may be positive and others negative in nature, but all these projections need to be let go in order to grow spiritually.

When I was in high school, it would drive me nuts that my friends would see my parents as being cool, while I was embarrassed to be seen with them. My parents could push me over the top in under a minute. But even though I wished my parents would crawl under a rock, I would fly into a rage if anyone criticized or made an off-color comment about either of them. It goes without saying that I had some serious ego projections with regard to my mother and father. These projections were not rational and they often conflicted with each other. They denied me a truly intimate relationship with either of them and seemed to spill over into my other relationships as well. As I began to apply the principles of yoga to my relationship with each of them, I noticed a few important changes. First, they were not as bad as I thought. Of course they have their struggles in life—as we all do—but they are not the monsters that I once thought they were. I have also found that my love for both of them has begun to assert itself, and I have stopped placing so many conditions on that love.

I was part of the generation that grew up on The Brady Bunch. As I sat and watched this show each night while my mother made dinner, I started to recognize a stark contrast between the way Mike and Carol Brady interacted with each other and their children and the way my family functioned. For years I held bitterness toward my parents for not being more like Mike and Carol Brady. When I finally stopped projecting the Brady Bunch dynamic onto them, I started to see them in a clearer light. As a matter of fact, I am grateful to have the parents I have. The family portrayed in the Brady Bunch was about as synthetic as the fake grass in their back yard. Growing up in a family like that would have been a real disaster.

To apply the practice of yoga to the relationship with parents, it is important to recognize that much of what we see in our parents is, in fact, not there. Once we recognize this we can begin to withdraw that ego projection and see them less and less as 'parents' and more and more as individuals. This is not easy, of course, because we have been projecting onto our parents longer than we've been projecting onto anyone else. Even though this is a difficult process, it is very important because the relationship we have with our parents becomes

the template where we build most of our other relationships. Once we withdraw the projections we have about our parents, our other relationships begin to heal as well.

Children

I can still hear my mother saying, "You are a reflection on me!" in one of her tirades, which were usually inspired by my behavior in high school. I always thought this was an odd statement, and I still tease her about it today, but many parents feel this way. They see their children as extensions of themselves rather than as individuals. When a person has or adopts a child, the temptation to project an ego onto that being is extremely great. This is why the ultimate spiritual practice is to be a conscious parent. It's one of the most difficult things in the world to allow yourself to be loving and supportive while recognizing that this being, your child, is not a possession.

A few years back my friend Jasper was visiting with his son, Bodhi. At the time, Bodhi was four years old. One of the things that impressed me most about Jasper was his commitment to conscious parenting.

While they were visiting, Bodhi and his father were wrestling and having fun until Bodhi twisted his arm. At first it seemed to be no big deal, but as a few more hours passed, his arm continued to hurt. It became apparent that he needed to see a doctor. Like many of us, Bodhi was not too keen about going to the emergency room. Rather than just make him go, kicking and screaming, Jasper sat him down and let him know that he had a choice. He gave him information and encouragement and helped him to muster up his courage. Seeing his son in pain was not easy for Jasper, and the temptation to take control and fix the immediate problem must have been great, but by letting Bodhi have a voice, Jasper helped him to find his own source of courage and strength.

While we were in the emergency room, another set of parents were bringing their daughter in. It was not clear exactly what had happened, but it appeared as if the little girl had fallen and needed stitches for a cut she had above her eye. The little girl was understandably frightened, but rather than empower her and let her have a voice, her mother responded to her protests with, "You're going to see a doctor and that's the end of it." Her mother meant well, of course, but in her fear, she was not able to let her daughter work through her own fears.

Conscious parenting is a full time practice. There is not a moment when part of the mind is not reaching out to the child. Reaching out to a child and offering love and support can be done without ego projection, however. As hard as this seems, it is the key to being a conscious parent.

Applying the principles of yoga to children is not easy because it means constantly letting go of control in precisely the place where it is most tempting to cling and hold. Clinging to children will not serve them and will only prevent the parent from seeing their unique beauty. While a parent is bonded with the child in such a way that love is inevitable, it is not a given that they see the child truly. In fact, that bond can be so strong that it makes it more difficult to see clearly. It's like pressing your face up against the TV screen and trying to see a meaningful image.

Therefore, the parent has the unique challenge of maintaining that sacred and intimate bond, while at the same time stepping back and seeing things as they are. This can be a very difficult practice, but in my observations, it is the best path available to an urban mystic.

Lovers

One of my longtime students, Rudy, had not been around for a while, and I began to wonder what had happened. He was very committed to his yoga practice and had come faithfully every day, so it was odd that I had not seen him. Eventually I bumped into him on the street and he told me that he had met a great guy, fallen in love, and the relationship was taking up a lot of his time. He had that foolish look of infatuation in his eyes that made me realize he was high on puppy love. Most of us know the feeling. It's a wonderful (and awesome) time when the whole world seems to be a bit brighter and you can't help but smile. While it is wonderful, it's a terrible time to make decisions of any importance. It's at this point that a spiritual practice is most needed to bring some clarity and groundedness to the relationship. Unfortunately, this is the time when most people do what Rudy did. They stop practicing altogether.

The problem with puppy love and romantic relationships in general, is that they are built on shabby spiritual foundations. Most people hope to find that perfect mate to make life complete. They believe that finding this seemingly perfect partner will result in living happily ever after, and that is simply not the case. After the honeymoon the work begins, and without a regular spiritual practice of some sort, there will be a rocky road.

Disney and the Grimm brothers were smart to end their stories with the Prince and the Princess riding off into the sunset. This ensures that all the endings are happy. After the sunset comes the work, and if you don't have your spiritual roots firmly established, that happy ending could quickly turn into a Greek tragedy.

Part of the problem starts before two people even meet. Most people are looking for a partner who will complete them. Their egos design the perfect mate, who will become an emotional caulking gun to seal up a cold and drafty heart. They then go looking for a mate on whom they can project these ego creations. There are two reasons why this can never work. First, seeking wholeness outside can only prevent you from finding it within. And second, no one can fit your ego's ideals all the time. Even if you find the seemingly perfect mate, you will ultimately grow to resent that person for not filling the void and meeting all of your ego expectations.

A more spiritually sound approach to a romantic relationship would be to find wholeness within first, and to become completely content with being alone. Once that foundation is in place you may find a person with whom to share part of your life. The key is to become Mr. or Ms. Right yourself, rather than trying to find that person outside you.

I don't know whether Rudy and his boyfriend will continue to be happy together. In the short term they are very full of love. My hope for them is that they may sustain that love by developing a spiritual practice together that will keep their young love fresh and new. When you consider the depth and beauty of the human soul, it's amazing that people grow bored and tired with each other, but it will be impossible to sustain a loving and ever-changing relationship when it's not spiritually grounded.

Sadhana Partners

Perhaps the most unique addition to intimate relationships that yoga offers is what I call the sadhana partnership. As we noted in the last chapter, sadhana means, "spiritual practice." For those of us who choose to make yoga our sadhana, this usually includes poses, breathing, and meditation techniques. Of course each person is different and their individual needs and tastes can help to create a unique sadhana.

Having a daily spiritual practice is an important part of living a centered life, but it can be very easy to get distracted by life in the urban world. That is why it is very helpful to find some sort of support. Many people find this support in the context of a yoga class, or by getting more involved with a local yoga studio. Others find it helpful to go to class with a friend. These are all ways of cultivating sadhana partners.

When I was still in college studying social work, I met a man named Michael. I was working in a coffeehouse at the time, and he would come in each day to buy the darkest roast coffee we had brewing. He always wore a nice suit, and his hairstyle was very short and clean-cut. We would often talk when he came in, and although we were very different people, there was an instant rapport that developed between us. On one of his visits to the coffeehouse, I shared with him that I had just been on a weekend yoga retreat, and this intrigued him. He asked me many questions that day about yoga and meditation, and I offered to teach him some basic yoga poses and meditation techniques.

That was the beginning of one of my closest friendships in this life. Michael was my first sadhana partner. Eventually Michael and I became roommates, which raised the eyebrows of my friends as well as his. No one knew exactly what to do with this seemingly mismatched living situation we had created. We were like the nineties version of the classic TV series the Odd Couple. He would iron everything, and I would barely take the time to fold my clothes and put them away. I had long hair and preferred to walk around barefoot as often as possible; Michael kept his hair closely cropped and always dressed like he was going for the most important job interview of his life. While I spent my days slinging coffee for the artsy East Side of Providence, Michael spent his days working in hotel sales.

The fact that we lived together with relatively few conflicts was nothing short of a miracle, and both of us attribute it to the one thing that we both shared. Each morning we would get up early to practice yoga and meditate together. Although we were both very different, we were both committed to the practice and this made our morning sadhana very magical. Some mornings Michael would lead the practice—other mornings I would lead. Occasionally we would do our own individual practice in silence.

Michael and I refer to that time in our lives as 'Hillside Ave.', after the street our apartment was on. There is not much more that can be said because the experience changed us both in such indescribable ways. In fact, I grew more during the time that Michael and I lived and practiced together than almost any other time in my life.

What happened for Michael and me can happen with any two people, or even a group of people. When we find a friend or group of friends that we can practice with, whether by going to a yoga class or by coming together for a less formal and impromptu practice, we transcend the limits of our individual wills, and oftentimes cultivate very intimate relationships. As we shall see in Part Two of this book, yoga works to heal the deepest levels of the mind, and sharing that practice with others is incredibly bonding. This is why so many romantic partners find that yoga brings their relationship to a new level.

Michael and I are currently neighbors in San Francisco. He still keeps his hair short and irons all his clothes. I still look and dress like a throwback from the sixties. But he is family to me now, and when life gets difficult, he's one of the first people I call, because he has seen me in my most vulnerable state. Our relationship goes way beyond most of my other relationships because he knows me in a way that few other people do.

The decision to work with another person can take many forms, and it is not a prerequisite for growth in the practice of yoga but it can be a major tool. I have found my sadhana partners to be more supportive in my practice than any block, strap or bolster ever could, because the real shifts that yoga inspires are internal ones. Having a friend or group of friends who support you in this process can make the difference between a spiritual life that is filled with struggle and one that flows smoothly.

Nemesis

The other day I turned on the news and was bombarded by coverage of the Timothy McVeigh execution. This type of emotionally charged event is a feeding frenzy for the media, and they took great pains to interview as many people as possible who had been affected by the bombing of the federal building in Oklahoma City. As one might expect, a lot of the survivors and relatives of the victims were still in a great deal of pain. Their reactions ranged from rage to great grief, which is all very understandable. One woman's statements stood out more than the others did, though. She had lost a loved one in the bombing and was invited to see the execution. She declined, saying that she had forgiven Timothy McVeigh for what he had done and had no desire to see him put to death.

What was most unique about this woman was not her words, but rather her peace. No doubt she still grieved, but she was not torn apart by emotion. She did not condone McVeigh's actions or even suggest that he receive a lighter sentence. She had simply let go of the full-time job of hating him, and in doing that she found peace. Her peace was such a ray of light in that newscast, and I hope that other survivors saw it.

This woman is extraordinary. I don't know that I have her capacity to forgive, but I do share her conviction that hating an enemy will not serve anything except perhaps to rob our peace of mind. There's a saying in Alcoholics Anonymous that goes, "Holding a resentment is like taking poison and hoping the other person dies." Yoga would have us refrain from taking that poison.

Having a nemesis is one of the ego's favorite ways of propagating the illusion of separation. Whenever we see people as the enemy, we are choosing not to see Atman in them; and when we deny it in them, we deny it in ourselves. This makes for a very difficult situation, because hate is much easier than love, and violence is much more stimulating than peace. A quick look at the TV guide will demonstrate what sells. Programs with violence and backstabbing get the ratings.

I don't envy the people who were affected by Timothy McVeigh's actions. They have a very difficult practice in front of them. Forgiving McVeigh may seem like a sellout and a sign of weakness because of the magnitude of his crime, but holding onto bitterness toward him would be to accept that violence into their own hearts.

There is a story about the Buddha that demonstrates this idea quite well. It concerns a wealthy merchant who had two sons. The younger of the two sons heard the Buddha speak and was so inspired by his kindness and wisdom that he decided to leave his father's home and follow the Master. This enraged the father who viewed the Buddha as a religious fanatic, so he sent his older son to go after his brother and bring him home. When the son finally caught up with his younger brother, he tried to bring him home, but his brother would not hear of it. Finally, the younger brother convinced him to hear the master speak once, and if he did not approve of his decision, he would go home without a fight. The older brother agreed to these terms, but when he heard the Buddha speak, he too was so moved that he renounced his life and followed with his brother. Naturally the father was furious, and he decided to take matters into his own hands. He sought out the Buddha to give him a piece of his mind.

When he finally found the great teacher, he shook his fists and yelled with rage, "Who do you think you are? You have stolen my two sons from me. I have no one to take over the family business and no one to care for me in my old age. How dare you call yourself a spiritual teacher!"

The Buddha looked calmly at him; his eyes filled with compassion and he said, "If a man offers you a gift and you refuse it, what becomes of the gift?" The father was confused, as this was not how he had expected their conversation to go. Still, he answered, "The gift would remain with the person who was trying to give it."

"That is correct," replied the Buddha. "I do not accept your gift of anger, but if you choose, I will show you the way to let it go and find peace." The man surrendered and became a follower of the Buddha that very day.

This is how we turn our relationships with our enemies into a yoga practice. By not accepting the gift of anger, fear and attack, we stop the spread of violence. By demonstrating peace, we offer an alternative to living in rage.

Judy and Dennis Shepard are excellent examples of this. Their son, Matthew Shepard, was beaten and left to die on a rural road in Wyoming because he was gay. Judy and Dennis have gone out of their way to make sure that his killers are treated fairly and they oppose the death penalty. (www.matthewsplace.com)

Rather than turn their pain and grief into an excuse to become bitter and depressed, they have used them to fuel their campaign for equal rights for the LGBT community. Their example is something that I use as a model for how we can all use our so-called negative relationships as a powerful spiritual practice, and an intimate part of our lives as modern yogis.

PART TWO

"Be fearless and pure; never waver in your determination
or your dedication to the spiritual life.
Give freely. Be self-controlled, sincere, truthful, loving,
and full of the desire to serve.
Realize the truth of the scriptures;
learn to be detached and to take joy in renunciation.
Do not get angry or harm any living creature,
but be compassionate and gentle; show good will to all.
Cultivate vigor, patience, will, purity; avoid malice and pride.
Then, Arjuna, you will achieve your divine destiny."

—BHAGAVAD GITA 16:1-3

CHAPTER FIVE

YAMA
the Moral Restraints

"Yoga perishes by these six: overeating, overexertion, talking too much, performing needless austerities, socializing and restlessness."

—HATHA YOGA PRADIPIKA 1:15

MORALITY

"Those who violate these laws, criticizing and complaining, are utterly deluded. They are the cause of their own suffering."
—BHAGAVAD GITA, 3:32

Yoga is a very practical practice. While its goals are lofty, it is a practice that starts where we are and builds on that foundation.

Learning to live fully in the world provides a space in which we can cultivate our spiritual practice and delve deeper into the heart and soul of our being.

In the yogic tradition there are five moral principles, known as the yamas, or restraints. Collectively they make up the first of the eight limbs outlined by Patanjali in his Yoga Sutra. They are ahimsa (nonviolence), satya (truthfulness), asteya (nonstealing), brahmacharya (sexual moderation), and aparigraha (greedlessness).

In many ways they resemble the Ten Commandments laid out by Moses in the book of Exodus, but most modern practitioners of yoga implement them in a decidedly different fashion than the way most Jews and Christians observe the Ten Commandments.

Most moral codes, such as the Ten Commandments, are viewed in a very black and white way. For instance, lying is wrong. End of story. There is no room for discussion or growth on this principle. Either you're telling the truth or you're lying.

The five restraints of yoga on the other hand are not about moral law. They are part of a practice, and as such are always being perfected. From a yogic point of view, you never stop trying to deepen your understanding and your implementation of the five restraints. Instead, you continue to examine your thoughts, beliefs and actions to see how and where you can take each of these restraints to a more profound level. (Not so black + white → Always keep working)

In many ways this can be liberating because it allows us to let go of guilt. When things are too black and white, guilt and feelings of inadequacy are sure to follow, for very few of us can be completely nonviolent or completely honest all the time. Because we feel such guilt, we often rationalize our behavior in an effort to minimize these uncomfortable feelings, and this allows us to continue and may even encourage us to live on morally shaky ground.

When we start taking a more yogic approach to morality, it becomes a practice, and in each situation in which we find ourselves, we have the opportunity to look at our behavior and decide how we can make it align more fully with our goals as an urban mystic. There is no room for guilt here, but plenty of room for growth.

For example, if a man feels guilty for cheating on his spouse, he is likely to look for reasons why this behavior is not so bad. Perhaps he will project some of the blame onto his wife for her disinterest in sex. Or perhaps he will share some of his guilt with his lover for being so sexy. He may even project his guilt onto his male gender, saying, "Boys will be boys."

Now if this same man were looking at his situation as a yogic practice, he would be able to look at the many ways he could deepen his understanding of Self. Rather than project the blame out, he can now take responsibility for his choices. The five yamas will offer him a standard on which to base his life and his actions, creating an opportunity to modify his behavior while simultaneously creating more space in his life for spiritual exploration. He can be more honest with himself, his wife and his lover, and he can begin to make choices that will be less hurtful to himself and others.

The important thing is that there is a choice. Because of the guilt imposed by strict moral codes, we project responsibility outward. Once we begin to let go of guilt and rigidity, we can again stand in our power to choose. Rather than feeling like a victim of the world, we can own our lives and our choices, and when a certain behavior is not working, we can choose differently.

This conscious decision-making with regard to our behavior is how we practice the moral restraints of yoga. By simply asking ourselves over and over again how we can be less violent or more honest, we begin to make changes and our lives begin to run more smoothly.

KARMA

"Those who live in accordance with these divine laws without complaining, firmly established and safe, are released from karma."
—BHAGAVAD GITA, CHAPTER 3:32

Karma is one of those over-used buzz words that make many people cringe. When it is properly understood, it can help us to make wise and informed choices in the world. Understanding this basic law is fundamental to working with the yamas if we are to use them in a way that is liberating rather than as a weapon of guilt.

The law of karma or cause and effect is really quite simple. It is the spiritual equivalent to Isaac Newton's law of motion— "Every action has an equal and opposite reaction."

The law of karma when properly understood is quite liberating because it puts the physical universe in our hands to mold and shape. Our lives become a canvas where we can paint whatever we like, but the key is to do this consciously.

Most of us react to life. We respond to each situation with a behavior or pattern that we learned in the past. This is why history always seems to repeat itself and why we seem to hit the same blocks over and over again in relationships, work and personal growth. Working through karma is the process of letting go of old patterns in behavior and thinking and allowing our spirit to replace that pattern with something more suited to our evolution.

Remember that yoga is a science. And as such the laws that guide it are universal and unconditional. Karma is one such law. We cannot stop this law, or find a place in all of time and space where it is not present, any more than we can stop the wind from blowing. But through the practice of yoga we can learn to use karma to sail through life, and when we get really talented, we can learn to use yoga to sail against the force of karma in much the same way a sailor can tack against the wind.

We take control of our own Lives

The urban mystic needs to develop a working understanding of karma if he or she is to really evolve. If every cause has an effect and every action has a reaction, then learning how to use the law of karma is essential. The first step in this process is changing our behavior to create a life that will support our spiritual growth.

All action begins at the level of the mind. It is the mind that tells the mouth to speak words of venom or words of kindness. It is the mind that tells the arms to strike or to embrace, and it is the mind that tells the legs to run in fear or to dance with joy. The good news is that we can change our minds at any point. We can explore the areas where we are stuck and then learn a new way of thinking that will free us to experience our divine nature more fully.

When I first stopped drinking and using drugs, I was a very bitter young man. I unconsciously blamed God for everything that was wrong with my life. I was unable to see that most of my difficulties in this world were the direct result of my own thoughts and actions. Until that point, I did not really understand the law of karma that governs this physical universe. I thought the universe owed me something and that I was being cheated because I had been dealt such a difficult hand in life.

In time I changed my mind, and my behavior followed. I began to see that my thoughts and behaviors were my greatest enemies in life, and with that awareness I began to change. Prior to that I would blame my teachers for my failing grades or my parents for my 'difficult' home life. This, of course, served no purpose except to project my responsibility outward, and to keep me stuck in patterns of behavior that were killing me.

Before we can explore each of the five yamas, we need to clarify one more thing. An urban mystic tries to let go of the idea that observing a moral code will make a person 'good' and not observing a moral code will make a person 'bad.' Every being is Atman and as such, no thought or behavior can make you more than what you are and no thought or behavior can diminish your innate value. The divine spark in Hitler was just as bright and full of potential as it was in Mother Theresa. The difference is that she was aware of it. She experienced that joy in her life and inspired it in others.

You are a complete spark of the divine. Living a more moral life will not change this one basic Truth. It will, however, make it much easier to realize this divine nature more fully, and that is where we begin to feel whole and complete.

I once heard a saying that resonated deeply for me. "We are not punished for our sins; we are punished by our sins." This sums up the yogic take on morality. A yogi doesn't practice the restraints to win God's favor or to avoid punishment in a future life. He cleans up his or her behavior to create space for deeper spiritual seeking.

Now, let's turn our awareness to the five moral restraints that make up the first limb of yoga.

———— **NONVIOLENCE (AHIMSA)** ————

Being firmly grounded in nonviolence creates an atmosphere in which others can let go of their hostility.—Yoga Sutra 2:35

The world can be a very violent place. So often I pick up the paper and feel the sensation of molten lead beginning to fill my heart and belly. My initial response is to judge the people who have behaved defiantly enough to make the front page of the paper. But the real reason for my heavy heart and judgmental attitude is because I am much more like the deviants making the front page than I am like one of the great yogis.

Granted, my ego boundaries will not allow me to commit some of the extremely violent acts that bombard our consciousness on a daily basis via the media, but I do harbor a deep-rooted violence at the subconscious level. Practicing ahimsa brings this violence into the light of awareness so that it can be neutralized.

Just as I finished college, I thought it would be a great idea to go on a meditation retreat. I chose what I thought would be a doable ten-day retreat. Upon entering this retreat, I agreed to maintain silence, to meditate for ten hours a day, and to abstain from reading, writing, and any contact with the outside world.

At this point in my life I had done a lot of meditation, and I knew that this would not be easy. But I was not expecting the barrage of violent thoughts that surfaced. It felt like there was a werewolf living inside me that was looking for any excuse to come out and rip me (and anyone else in his path) to shreds.

In the months that followed, I contemplated what had happened. Ironically, the experience of facing my violent nature allowed me to transcend some of it and to live a more peaceful life. But a question haunted me: Why did experiencing such violence seem to free me from it? It was quite some time before I really understood the answer. I have come to realize that the reason why I don't experience this violence in my day-to-day life is because my ego has become very capable of projecting this violence outward onto others. Rather than look at it and let it go, I continually project it onto other people or institutions and thus skirt any responsibility for this rage.

For me, this comes out most clearly when I am behind the wheel of a car. Granted that I have managed to refrain from running someone off the road, but the words that come out of my mouth and the occasional hand gestures that fly outward from my mind are anything but nonviolent. In many ways it is the perfect place to project my violence with few repercussions on a social level.

The practice of ahimsa is not about denial of violence, but rather the transcending of it. On the one hand the urban mystic seeks to modify his or her behavior in order to create less violent situations in his or her life. But this is only the beginning of the practice. By simultaneously refraining from violent acts and looking at the unconscious thought patterns that inspire them, we become more peaceful, and our natural reaction to adversity will be peace rather than attack.

TRUTHFULNESS (SATYA)

"For those grounded in truthfulness,
every action and its consequences are imbued with truth."
—YOGA SUTRA 2:36

Satya is the practice of truthfulness. In its most basic form it is "not lying," but like ahimsa, it is a much greater practice for the dedicated urban mystic. The practice of satya involves an ever-deepening awareness of what Truth is. And so, before we can really explore what truthfulness is, we need to define Truth. This is no easy task, because you will rarely find two people who agree on exactly what Truth is. There are ideals, however, and that is what we will explore.

Any discussion on Truth needs to be preceded by a discussion on perception, for it is our perceptions that tell us what we believe to be true. Perception is the filter that exists between our senses and our mind. It's like a stained glass window that bends the light of Truth into many colors, but never lets in the complete light.

The colored glass of our perception is made up of our past experiences and our future projections. It is always false in the sense that some of the light will not make it through, and always partially true in the sense that some of the light will shine through. Learning to see the beauty of the glass, while at the same time recognizing that there is a limit to what we are seeing, is what satya is all about.

Yoga is largely the practice of healing our perceptions. Many of us have a very warped view of the world. As our senses scan our surroundings, we see shadows of our past experience everywhere. These shadows prevent us from seeing the joy and ecstasy present in every situation.

As we have stated numerous times, Atman is the Truth about who we are. In fact Atman is the Truth about all living things. When we let our perceptions define truth for us, we deny ourselves the opportunity to experience joy and ecstasy because we are denying our Self. This is why it is so important to heal our perceptions first and then begin to move beyond them.

There are two kinds of truth. The first is the most familiar. It's the kind we hear about when we are in a court of law. When you're asked to put your hand on a Bible and "tell the whole truth and nothing but the truth," you're being asked to recount facts in an honest way. This is truth with a small 't'. It's truth that is filtered through perception, but it is not outwardly deceptive.

The other kind of truth has a capital 'T'. This is the ultimate Truth that exists beyond our perceptions of time and space. It's this Truth that we seek to discover through our spiritual practice, and it is this experience of Truth in which we seek to ground ourselves.

To practice satya there are two things we need to consider. First, we need to practice truthfulness within the illusion. As we walk through our lives, we need to keep examining our communication with others. We need to ask ourselves, "Is this the most truthful way I can use my words?"

There is a wide spectrum to communication. On one extreme we find the outright lie; on the other end we find the complete and unabridged truth. In between these two points we find varying degrees of evasiveness. As yogis, we do not merely seek to live in the middle, because that would result in misleading people whenever things got uncomfortable. Rather, we seek to speak our truth and demonstrate it in our actions. This is not always easy, but it ultimately liberates us from the bondage of living under even the subtlest of false pretenses.

When practicing this form of truthfulness, we refrain from lying, gossiping, and using our words, gestures and facial expressions to deceive people or to convince someone that they are something they are not. It means using our words mindfully and doing our best not to cloud the truth.

I was in a business the other day, and a delivery truck was making a delivery. The truck was parked in such a way that it blocked the neighbor's driveway. She came into the store and politely asked the delivery man to move the truck, explaining that she was in a real hurry.

Both the delivery man and the manager of the business ignored her. It was as if she had not even spoken. She asked again this time politely, but with a bit more urgency in her tone. Still, she got no response. After her third request, the delivery man stormed out of the store and the manager yelled after the woman, "Thanks for your patience!" with a snooty and sarcastic attitude.

From my point of view as a casual observer, the whole scene was so surreal. There was no doubt that the delivery man had illegally parked, and was inconveniencing someone greatly as a result. Yet rather than use their words to heal the situation, they projected their discomfort back onto her by the way they moved and spoke.

A more yogic way to respond to this woman might be to acknowledge her. By using a look or a word or gesture at least to acknowledge the woman, these men would in essence be saying, "You are important and worth noticing." Further, they could have been more expeditious in their moving the truck. In this way they would convey the message that she had a voice and that her voice meant something. Lastly, the manager's words could have been delivered with sincerity and compassion rather than used to slap her in the face.

Satya begins with our words, but it doesn't end there. It is in the way we walk and the tone of our voice. It is in our facial expression and in our gestures. If Atman is the Truth about what each of us is, then satya is striving to bring that Truth closer and closer to our awareness. The beautiful gift of satya is that when we begin to be more truthful in our communications with others, we begin to be more truthful with ourselves, for satya is as much about the words we say to ourselves as the words we say to each other.

When I first started practicing satya, I was overwhelmed with self-judgment, because I realized that my words were so harsh. But in doing that I was defeating the whole purpose. You should try not to condemn yourself if your words are less than loving. Simply look at these words and smile, and then do your best to clean them up. Never forget that yoga is a practice.

As we clean up our words and practice satya in the world, we begin to realize Truth in the spiritual sense of the word. This in turn makes it easier and easier to speak words that heal, rather than build up walls between our minds.

NONSTEALING (ASTEYA)

*"For those who have no inclination to steal,
the truly precious is at hand."*
—YOGA SUTRA 2:37

When we practice ahimsa, our life becomes more peaceful because we take responsibility for violent thoughts. Likewise, when we practice satya (monitoring our thoughts, words and actions to see when we are expressing things that are less than truthful), we begin to realize our true nature as Atman. My hope is that you will have noticed a pattern developing, and as we will see, asteya is going to follow in the same vein.

Asteya is the practice of nonstealing. Like the previous yamas, it is much more than a black and white decree. It is a practice that needs to be lived in order for it to be deepened and cultivated. It is a practice that offers us a doorway out of scarcity.

Before we can really explore the practice of nonstealing, we need to look at the principles of abundance and scarcity. There are two approaches to living life. One approach is the belief that something is lacking, and the other is that life, by its very nature, is abundant.

The ego, or the part of our mind that believes that it is separate, small and finite, holds the scarcity principle as one of its chief tenets. To the ego, there is never enough. The ego is always feeling lack and projecting that experience of lack onto the outside world. We hear this all the time in statements like, "There just isn't enough money," or, "If I only had more time." Most of us have lived under scarcity for so long that we don't know any other way to be.

As a result, the ego is always trying to get more. Even when the economy is good and we have paychecks that are sizable, the ego ups our list of 'needs'. Have you ever stopped to notice that the bigger your paycheck gets, the bigger seem your bills? The new TV that you just can't live without feels like such a priority because the ego has convinced you once again that something outside yourself can satisfy that insatiable spiritual hunger that we want so desperately to go away.

When we approach life from the belief in scarcity, life mirrors that back to us. In that reflection we see a world that demands that we do things we hate in order to survive. For some, that is robbing the liquor store; for others, it is working as the CEO of a big company. But in either case, their actions are motivated by a belief that there is not enough, and that to survive in this world you need to fight to get ahead.

The practice of asteya asks us to avoid this type of thinking and to adjust our behavior accordingly. When we rob the bank or step on others to get ahead, our minds affirm the scarcity principle, and we sentence ourselves to a life of fear. Even if we surpass Bill Gates in wealth and power, we will live in fear of losing what we have.

This is true for the heart as well. Our popular culture demands that we hoard our love and affection. Love, if you believe everything you read on a greeting card, is a very limited resource. It is only to be given out when we are getting certain behaviors in return, and it must be given only to a choice few. This is, of course, completely untrue. The only lack of love in the world is the belief that the well of our hearts can ever run dry.

Our Spirit sees things in a very different way. There is no need to steal, because there is no need of anything on the spiritual level, except perhaps to extend. To the Spirit that dwells within each of us, the things in this physical world which seem to be needs are not needs at all. There will always be enough food and water and cellular telephones.

We, as a community, need to move beyond the idea of lack and start trusting in the idea of abundance.

Mother Theresa was once asked how she could take a pro-life stand on abortion when she could so clearly see all the children in the world who were suffering. Without thinking, she quickly replied, "The problem is not the children. The problem has never been the children. The problem is that people refuse to feed the children."

I don't share Mother Theresa's views on abortion, but I do agree that the problem of lack in this world is created by our belief in scarcity. There is plenty of food. There are plenty of hearts to love, and there is plenty of money to make it all happen. The problem is that we feel on a very deep level that if we were simply to give, we would not have enough for ourselves.

This false belief not only grinds national economies to a halt, it also inspires an experience of primal fear. Just as consumer confidence is one of the leading factors in a healthy economy, a personal sense of confidence that there will be enough of all that is needed (be it time, money or love) is the factor that creates space for the growth necessary if we want to realize our divine nature fully.

When we live under Spirit's law of abundance, many wonderful things begin to happen. We no longer feel trapped by our jobs. Rather, we can quit jobs that don't satisfy us and instead spend our time doing that which makes our heart sing. We no longer worry about paying the bills or have any desire to cheat or steal because there is an internal knowing that all we need will come to us.

This way of thinking is much more than a positive and optimistic attitude to wealth. I once read that Gandhi's mother ate less than a handful of rice each day, and did so by choice. She lived under the grace of abundance because she had all she needed and was content.

There are many people who are very wealthy and yet live in fear of a stock market crash or a hostile takeover.

Under Spirit's watchful eye, our relationships bloom. We are able to love freely, and our codependent and neurotic relationships are either healed or given up altogether. Our love addictions and our experiences of jealousy and insecurity begin to disappear, and we begin to realize the deep sense of intimacy that gives way to fast-track spiritual growth.

When Patanjali promises that abstinence from stealing will result in jewels showering down upon us, he means it quite literally. By recognizing that there is nothing to steal, on any level, we shift our thinking from one of scarcity to one of abundance, and the world opens to offer us wealth beyond the comprehension of the person caught in scarcity. This is what is offered us by the practice of asteya.

SEXUAL MODERATION (BRAHMACHARYA)

"The chaste acquire vitality."
—YOGA SUTRA 2:38

Brahmacharya, the fourth yama, is the practice of using one's sexual energy in a mindful and conscious way. While this can be done in several ways, it has traditionally been practiced by abstaining from sexual activity with others, as well as from masturbation.

In the not-so-distant past, a student of yoga would be asked to take strict vows of celibacy before he or she would even be considered for training. Of course, in many traditions this dissolved when yoga started to become more trendy here in the West. Liberal Americans and Europeans were not thrilled about the idea of letting go of their hard won sexual freedom, and so brahmacharya is rarely discussed in urban settings.

Before we get into the practice of brahmacharya, I think it is important to reaffirm the concept to which we have returned over and over again in this chapter—that the yamas are not about making a person good or bad. Yoga doesn't view sex as dirty and immoral or even as a bad thing. In fact, rather than denying or exploiting our sexuality, it sees it as a powerful force that should be used for our spiritual growth.

In order to understand the importance of brahmacharya, we need to review a concept from Chapter Three. As I noted in that chapter, kundalini energy lies dormant at the base of the spine, coiled like a sleeping serpent. On occasion, she wakes and begins her ascent up the spine until eventually she reaches the crown chakra where she is united with her formless lover.

When this ascension begins, we most often experience it as sexual arousal. Many of us have become quite adept at allowing this energy to rise up as high as the second chakra and then diffusing it outward by masturbating or having sex with another person. While there is certainly nothing wrong with sexual activity, it is important to remember that the traditional orgasm diffuses the sexual energy and greatly reduces the chances of it rising any higher than the second chakra.

All the forms of the practice of brahmacharya are about much more than simply changing our sexual behavior. They are more about changing our thinking around sexuality than about how we express it. Remember, thought directs both energy and behavior. By changing our minds about sex we simultaneously change our behavior and direct that energy in a more conscious way.

There are two main forms of brahmacharya. The first and more traditional form is celibacy. In this practice one abstains from sexual activity altogether. This includes abstaining from masturbation and sexual activities with others. This is not a denial of sexual energy. In fact, it is the practice of bringing heightened awareness to our sexuality.

When practicing yogic celibacy, a yogi begins to notice all the times that he or she is looking outside for fulfillment. Rather than foster those thoughts with fantasy or engaging in sexual activity, the energy is directed to the higher centers. Sexual thoughts and fantasies are bound to come up—and in the beginning will come up with a fury—but training the mind not to engage these thoughts (an activity which fuels them) creates space for other pursuits—namely moving the kundalini up the spine.

My friend Betsy once remarked that she had been celibate for quite a while. She had a crush on a male friend and he didn't seem to be returning her affections. For a month or more she had been flirting with him and trying to get his attention, but nothing seemed to work. Because he was not interested, she had gone for several months without sex. Although Betsy was not having sex, she was certainly not practicing brahmacharya, because brahmacharya is much more than a dry spell in the dating arena. If she were, she would have made a conscious decision not to engage in sexuality and she would have worked to curtail her flirting and fantasizing. The issue is not whether she actually had sex. For the amount of energy that she spent chasing after this guy, she might as well have been having sex. The issue here is how people direct their sexual energy and whether they do it consciously.

The second way a person can practice brahmacharya is through a conscious sexual relationship. This relationship can be between members of the same or opposite sex, and can have any number of styles such as monogamous or open. The relationship can be long-term or can be short-lived. The nature and style of the relationship is really not that important, though many people feel safer in a committed situation.

Again, what determines brahmacharya is what's in the mind. When two people come together for sex, one of two forces is always behind the act. The sexual energy will be used either by the ego or by Spirit. These are the only two motivators in any act, and sex is no different.

When a sexual relationship is driven by the ego, both people entering into the act want to get something. Perhaps one wants to use the other's body for physical pleasure, or perhaps there are unresolved issues from the relationship between one's parents. Even people who enter into sex in a more submissive role are often trying to get some kind of revenge, though they appear to be in the giving role.

When a sexual experience is motivated by Spirit, it is the act of giving. It's the experience of sharing and exchanging energy to coax both partners' kundalini higher and higher up the spine. As this happens, the sexual union becomes much more than a first chakra survival act or a second chakra erotic act. As kundalini ascends, each chakra along the way opens and resonates with the corresponding chakra belonging to his or her partner. When partners work together in a safe and conscious way, the kundalini energy can rise more freely. In fact, some forms of tantric yoga encourage couples to raise this energy together, and then create an inverted orgasm. In this experience a person pulls the energy in, rather than having a traditional outward orgasm.

The form of brahmacharya one chooses to practice is not all that relevant. Yogic celibacy and conscious relationships are both wonderful when practiced consciously, and both can be appropriate at different times in one's life. What is important is that we allow our sexual energy to be used on behalf of Spirit. When we do this we feel uplifted and cleansed by our sexual energy. When we let the ego drive our sexuality, we wind up repressing this vital energy, or exploiting it in a way that drains our energy and makes us feel spiritually depressed.

— GREEDLESSNESS (APARIGRAHA) —

"Freedom from wanting unlocks the real purpose of existence."
—YOGA SUTRA 2:39

Aparigraha is the practice of becoming greedless. On the surface it seems a bit easier than the other yamas, because being a greedy person is not a desirable trait. In fact our culture spares no expense in its attack on the greedy, saying that they should give more to the poor and that they don't deserve their wealth.

Of course, it is true that some people with vast amounts of wealth could and perhaps should give more to the less fortunate. It's important to remember, however, that the practice of yoga is not about what other people do, but rather about what we do as individuals. Like all the other yamas, becoming less greedy is a practice, and when we practice this yama, we are much less likely to project greed outward onto others.

Greed is an interesting thing because, like stealing, it affirms a sense of lack and scarcity. When a person comes from a place of greed, he or she must believe in lack, or the concept of greed would be meaningless. Therefore, it is in one's own self interest to consider this yama closely.

I went through most of college on grants and scholarships. When I was about three years into my studies, I ran out of money. No matter where I looked for money, I couldn't seem to find any. As the weeks went by, I realized that I had to drop out of school because I could not afford another semester.

At that time, I was also looking into massage school. I had sent away for information on several schools, but one appealed to me more than the others. In order to apply I needed to send them fifty dollars along with the application. As I had only seventy dollars in my account and no way of paying for my schooling even if I got accepted, it seemed like a waste of money.

Although the situation looked bleak, I put the application on my small altar during my afternoon meditation in hopes of some sort of guidance or inspiration. By the time I had finished my sit, I knew what I had to do. I wrote out the check, addressed an envelope and sent off the application.

On the way to the mailbox, I bumped into my friend and landlord Ed. I asked him to join me for dinner. Although I only had twenty dollars, I felt inspired. When the check came, Ed wanted to pay for his half of the meal, but I felt strongly that I should treat him despite my lack of funds. Although it was not an expensive meal, I left a generous tip. I figured that if my bank account was empty, things could only improve.

All of this 'irresponsibility' led to a great sense of peace and the knowledge that things would somehow work out. When I got home that night, my mother had left a message on my answering machine. She had just received a call from her real-estate agent. After sitting for over a year on the market, the house her aunt had left her had finally sold and she wanted to help me pay for my schooling.

For me, this was a strong affirmation of the importance of aparigraha. By opening up my wallet and offering to put my resources out there, I had created room for more abundance. I took a leap of faith in the renouncement of my money, but it somehow made way in my mind and heart for the work ahead of me.

When we practice aparigraha, we let selfishness be replaced by selflessness, and we allow the greed that is inspired by a fear of scarcity to be replaced by generosity. Just as still water becomes stagnant, hoarded resources become toxic to our souls. When we practice aparigraha we allow resources to flow through us, rather than allowing ourselves to block the flow of abundant energy that is always present.

Each one of these yamas—ahimsa (nonviolence), satya (truthfulness), asteya (nonstealing), brahmacharya (sexual moderation), and aparigraha (greedlessness)—works with all the others. They are like the threads of a spider web. When we practice one, all the others get engaged. When we consciously work these practices simultaneously, their effect on our lives is exponentially increased, creating a solid platform on which to practice yoga's seven remaining limbs.

CHAPTER SIX

NIYAMA
Observances

---

*"Unwholesome thoughts can be neutralized
by cultivating wholesome ones."*
—YOGA SUTRA 2:33

CULTIVATING GOOD HABITS

*"Yoga succeeds by these six: enthusiasm, openness, courage,
knowledge of the truth, determination and solitude."*
—HATHA YOGA PRADIPIKA 1:16

As we noted in the last chapter, the first limb of yoga (yama) begins with a moral code that is better viewed as a practice rather than a hard and fast line between right and wrong. The same idea is true for the second limb, niyamas.

Like the first limb, this second limb is made up of five practices. The niyamas are different from the yamas, however. While the yamas outline things that a yogi should avoid, such as lying and stealing, the niyamas speak of things we want to cultivate. That is why the niyamas are frequently referred to as the five observances. They are: shauca (purity), samtosha (contentment), tapas (austerity), svadhyaya (study), and ishvara pranidhana (surrender).

The niyamas are not practiced to make a person more spiritual or more holy. They are practiced to help us create a life where there is room for Spirit. The ego is very adept at filling our lives with all sorts of 'busyness' and toxic thinking, so we never have the chance to look at the important issues of Spirit. By practicing the niyamas, we consciously make space in our lives for the deeper spiritual pursuits in the yoga limbs that are to follow.

A few years back, when I was living in Montana, I was approached by one of my students who always seemed to have that star-struck look in her eyes whenever I was around. This often happens when a student confuses the teacher with the practice. A lot of people find immediate relief from their suffering and an instant sense of peace from their yoga practice. Sometimes they falsely associate yoga's success with their teacher.

I had just given a talk on living a pure life to support one's yoga practice, and she had a few questions. Because her questions were somewhat extensive I asked her to join me for dinner. She excitedly accepted, but looked as if there were a short circuit in her brain when I suggested that we go to Taco Bell. I guess she thought that because I was a yoga teacher that I had to live on tofu and brown rice, and that such a strict diet would make me more spiritual.

My whole reason for wanting to go to Taco Bell was not for the food per se. Rather, I was trying to demonstrate that I was human and that living a yogic life didn't mean you had to live a perfectly pure, austere existence. Of course, I try not to frequent fast food restaurants, and I do eat my fair share of tofu and brown rice, but I try not to make a religion out of living a clean lifestyle. Such an obsession only distracts from the upper limbs of yoga, rather than creating a foundation for them.

She and I became friends after that dinner, and would dine together after class on a regular basis. She was able to see me as a normal guy who tries to live a clean and healthy life. We even started going to the food co-op, where we could get all the organic health food a yogi could ask for.

When we practice the niyamas, it is tempting to think that living them perfectly will somehow make us more spiritual. This is far from the truth. Striving to work them fully into your life will assist your overall practice greatly, but they are not designed to bring about spiritual enlightenment, only to clear a space where a yogi can go deeper into the practice. I have met lots of people who follow the niyamas to the letter who are still unhappy; while others, who are not able to follow them well at all, seem very content. As with all things in yoga, balance and moderation are the key.

PURITY (SHAUCA)

"Purification also brings about clarity, happiness, concentration, mastery of the senses, and capacity for self-awareness."
—YOGA SUTRA 2:41

Shauca is the first niyama and it is the practice of keeping the body and mind pure. Ultimately, the practice of yoga is about removing the blocks to the awareness of our true nature—Atman. This is not an easy task because of our many attachments, and we often make things worse by piling on more blockages every day. This makes our yoga practice a system of maintenance rather than one of evolution. In the early stages of someone's yoga practice it is not uncommon for them to continue with their lifestyle unchanged. Because so many people live high-stress lives, their yoga practice is more about repairing the day-to-day damage inflicted by such a toxic lifestyle rather than about evolving and growing.

There usually comes a point in a person's yoga practice where the old way of living becomes less and less desirable, and the student wants to make changes in diet, occupation and/or relationships. Until a person does this, it is an uphill battle. The yoga practice may slow the bleeding, but it won't heal the wound unless we stop re-opening it with unhealthy lifestyle habits. This is where the practice of Shauca becomes so essential to our overall yoga practice.

Shauca is the practice of living a more pure life. It is applied to several areas of a yogi's lifestyle. Its sole purpose is to help us cease from putting garbage into the mind and body, and so give us a fair shake at removing the stuff that is already there. When I first started practicing yoga, I was a two to three pack-a-day smoker. I loved my cigarettes, but they made my yoga practice quite painful. Pranayama seeks to use the breath to fill the body with oxygen, among other things. The breathing techniques I was learning were no doubt helping to clear my lungs and give my body and mind some much-needed oxygen, but I was never able to move deeply into the pranayama part of my yoga practice, because every day I was dumping more toxins into my lungs than the poses and breathing could purge.

When I quit smoking, my yoga practice hit a new level. Now that my lifestyle supported my practice I could feel the awesome effects of the breathing techniques. I was moving forward with my spiritual and physical health, rather than simply treading water or sinking a bit more slowly.

The practice of shauca is applied to three basic areas of life. They are diet, intoxicants and mental stimulation. All day long we allow things to enter our bodies and minds in these three areas. Each is different, but they all share one quality: in each area the things we choose to take in have a dramatic effect on how deep our practice will be. Of course, anyone who practices yoga will benefit from the experience even without cleaning up these areas of his or her life, but not purifying the lifestyle is like trying to run a race in high heels. You could do it, but it would be difficult and inefficient. Therefore, let's take a look at each of these important areas.

A perfect diet is not a requirement for spiritual growth, but it certainly helps to eat foods that are clean and healthy. Eating a high fat, unbalanced diet affects our minds and our bodies, so it is very helpful to cut out certain foods and reduce others.

Things like white sugar and caffeine make meditation very difficult and they don't do the immune system any favors either. Animal products tend to be high in saturated fats and more difficult to digest. Animal products also tend to be heavy on the system and can keep the mind anchored in the lower chakras. Therefore, for many yogis a vegetarian diet is standard. Of course, not all yogis become vegetarians, but conscious eating is almost essential; keeping the diet light is a major asset. In addition, it is recommended that a yogi not only pay attention to what is eaten, but also to the quality of the food that is taken in. Four thousand years ago, when yoga was forming, organic was not an issue, as all food was natural. Now, however, it is a big issue. Therefore, it is helpful to eat organic, whole foods whenever possible.

The idea is to give the body as much nutrition and prana as possible, while taxing it as little as possible. When we eat a high fat diet that is filled with pesticides and artificial ingredients, we tax our bodies and create ill health. The energy that it takes to repair such damage could otherwise have been used on our spiritual practice.

While not all yogis abstain from alcohol, tobacco, caffeine and recreational drugs, it is a good idea to eliminate or limit these things.

In addition to the physical risks associated with drugs, alcohol, caffeine and tobacco, they also affect the mind dramatically. Since in yoga we are working to change and purify the mind, it makes no sense to dump toxins into it faster than a yoga practice can clear them out.

Traditionally, a yogi would have to take a vow to abstain from intoxicants before he or she would even be considered as a student; however, many modern yogis find it acceptable to drink or use drugs socially. While I don't personally feel that the social use of intoxicants is a terrible thing, I do feel that the use of intoxicants is quite inhibiting to yoga practice. It is for this reason that I encourage my students to abstain from such substances or, at most, to use them rarely.

It's not only our bodies that can take things in. In fact, our minds can be the most difficult place to practice Shauca. All day long we are bombarded with mental stimuli, which, for better or for worse, get filtered into our minds.

We find these stimuli in the music we listen to and in the websites we visit. TV, radio and the mass media play a huge part too. The yogis of the past could never have imagined the things to which our modern world exposes us. This makes it all the more important that we bring mindfulness to the things we put into our minds.

After the Columbine High School massacre in Colorado I read an article stating that the average child would see over 18,000 murders on TV and in movies before high school graduation. That is an astounding number and not just a little bit sick. While children are a bit more open to taking in such things, they are not alone. As adults, we also take in everything we see, hear and read. All of this stimulus is a lot to deal with, and it makes it that much harder for us to sink to the depths to which yoga is calling us.

Living in our modern world, it's hard to imagine a life without most of the things mentioned above. When I travel it is especially difficult to keep my diet clean; every billboard I drive by and every magazine I pick up is filled with stimuli for my mind that, as a yogi, I would rather not take in. Because of this, I have found it is necessary to cut myself some slack. I do my best to eat healthy and monitor what I take into my mind. When I do need to stray a bit, I try to bring mindfulness to it. I try not to judge or rationalize the behavior, but just look at it for what it is. I have found that practicing Shauca in this way allows me to keep my life clean most of the time while giving myself enough wiggle room for my modern urban life.

———— SAMTOSHA (CONTENTMENT) ————

"Contentment brings unsurpassed joy."
—YOGA SUTRA 2:42

The second niyama is samtosha, which is the practice of contentment. When I first learned about this niyama, I thought it sounded weird. Contentment was something I had experienced from time to time. Often it was something that seemed to be a result of my hatha yoga practice. But it was not something I consciously chose. It always seemed to be something that sort of just happened.

This is where yoga heaps a large responsibility on our shoulders. Most of us go through life waiting for the right situation to make us content. The standard American dream is one where you're popular in high school, go to a great college, marry the perfect spouse, have two-point-five children, retire and die in the arms of your loving husband or wife. There is nothing wrong with holding this, or any other, vision as your life's ambition. The problem arises when we attach our capacity for contentment to such goals.

Yoga teaches us to choose contentment in every moment, regardless of what is before us. Viewing contentment as a choice is nothing less than a radical notion. Virtually everything we are taught causes us to believe that contentment is condition-based and in order to find it you need to do or acquire certain things.

It is the very belief that contentment is the prize for winning the scavenger hunt of life that prevents us from being content. Once again, the ego has taken one of our natural desires and turned it into a weapon to prevent our waking up.

The practice of samtosha involves several steps. First, it is essential to be in the present moment. The limbs I will discuss in the next few chapters will greatly help to refine this present mindedness, but even in the early stages of a person's yoga practice it is important to start coming to the moment rather than dwell in the past or project into the future.

The second step is to notice your judgments about whatever is going on in the present moment. Perhaps you are happy and satisfied or maybe you're uncomfortable and anxious. Whatever you may be experiencing on a physical, emotional or psychological level, just note it and bring your focus to where you are. This is not always easy because we often bury our true feelings and judgments, but this is an essential step toward finding contentment.

The third and final step is to make peace with what is. We will learn more about this process as we continue our journey through the eight limbs of yoga, but even early on we can become aware of a conscious choice for peace and contentment over drama and conflict. This choice for contentment must happen in the present moment. As long as you believe that contentment will happen sometime down the road, you will never find it.

This doesn't mean we don't take steps to change an unhealthy situation. On the contrary, being content in this moment creates the space and the mindfulness to make more and healthier choices about life. Until we choose contentment in the present moment, we will likely make decisions based on the drama of the ego, and that is the quickest way to create situations that help us to rationalize our discontent.

In October of 1999, my sister was in a very bad car accident. She was in Hartford, Connecticut, at the time, and I was living in San Francisco. I first got the call from my father who was on his way to the hospital. He didn't have much information, and only knew that she was in critical condition and that she was going in for immediate surgery. He promised to call when he knew something more.

I felt like someone had just hit me with a stun gun. I wanted to cry or scream or something, but I was in complete overwhelm. It was Halloween night, and I had some friends over. We were putting on our costumes when I got the call. I tried to go back to the festivities, but couldn't keep myself focused, so I decided to sit and meditate for a bit. As I sat, I tried to practice samtosha.

At first it was hard. My mind was torn between dwelling on my sister's condition and the sense that I should have been in the other room, playing host to my friends. But I did my best to focus on my breath. As I did this, I allowed myself to enter more and more into the present moment. My projections and assumptions about what might happen with my sister were brought to a slow murmur.

By coming to the present moment I was able to let go of my fears about my sister's future well-being. Prior to that, my ego kept planning her funeral and other frightful renditions of the worst-case scenario, making contentment and clear perception of the situation impossible.

I then explored my feelings about the situation. I was very scared, but I was also very grateful that she was still alive. It could have been much worse. This step also brought me closer to peace. Once I stopped projecting my own fears onto her situation, I was able to feel my feelings and to recognize that I had a choice.

Once I recognized that I had a choice, I was able to find a sense of contentment—at least for the moment. I knew there was nothing I could do but pray. Over the next few weeks I would struggle a lot with the practice of samtosha. My sister's condition did improve over time, and while she still has some physical problems as a result of the accident, she is in great shape. And even though she pulled through, each phone call I got updating me on her condition was an opportunity to work samtosha.

In some cases, it may be helpful to sit and meditate when trying to choose contentment. But that is not always practical. Choosing contentment is something we want to do in each breath. As we learn to work the above three steps, choosing contentment will become a natural response to anything that throws us off center. Ten years ago, a traffic jam or a late bus would have ruined my whole day. I am still not above losing my peace of mind over such things, but I am much quicker to choose contentment when this type of thing happens. Because I try to practice samtosha with the little day-to-day things, I am much more prepared for the bigger things when they come around.

One of the ways we prepare to practice samtosha in life is through hatha yoga. When you come to a pose that is difficult, it is tempting to give up and stop trying, or to compare yourself to the person next to you, or to convince yourself that you will be happy when you perfect the pose. But by staying present in the pose, and choosing contentment with where the body is, we make space for growth. When we stay stuck in judgment and anxiety about our physical limitations, we not only cheat ourselves out of contentment in the moment, we deny ourselves the space to move forward with the practice.

TAPAS (AUSTERITY)

"As intense discipline burns up impurities,
the body and its senses become supremely refined."
—YOGA SUTRA 2:43

Tapas is the third niyama. It is the practice of creating an austere life. Austerity is simplicity through modest living. Traditionally, a yogi would renounce the world altogether, letting go of all worldly possessions except perhaps a loincloth and a rice bowl. Once again, this would be impractical for most of us. But this doesn't mean that the practice of tapas can't be modified for the urban mystic.

There is a story from India of a very wealthy man who lived in a great mansion with many rooms. He was a generous and good man who was very devoted to his spiritual practice. Although he had many servants and fine clothes, he placed his spiritual practice above all else.

There was an old yogi who lived nearby and had heard about this man who claimed to be spiritual, but would not let go of his worldly possessions. The yogi himself had only a rice bowl and the loincloth that he wrapped around his waist. The yogi decided that he would pay this man a visit to show him the error of his ways.

When he arrived at the rich man's mansion, he was greeted warmly. The two sat and meditated and then chatted for hours about the nature of Spirit and other related topics. While they were in the middle of their conversation, however, a fire broke out in the mansion. One of his servants came in and informed the master of the house that he would need to evacuate.

Because he was enjoying his conversation so much, the man declined, but agreed to move to a different wing of the house. As the fire continued to spread, his servant again encouraged them to evacuate. Again the man refused, but moved to yet another wing of the mansion. Finally the rich man and the yogi were forced to escape with only enough time to see the large home disappear in smoke and ashes. The wealthy man calmly turned to the yogi to continue their conversation, but the old yogi just lay on the ground and sobbed.

"What's wrong?" asked the rich man.

"I lost my rice bowl in the fire. Now I have nothing."

Of course the moral to this story is that having a lot doesn't mean you can't practice tapas, and having a little doesn't necessarily mean you're practicing it well. I think, as urban mystics, we can glean a lot of wisdom from this story.

Because most of us are called to live in the world, we will need some possessions. Even as I write this, I am typing into a two thousand-dollar computer system. Having possessions or not having possessions is not the issue. The core of tapas is whether or not those possessions help us to live a more centered life.

This is a difficult call, because the ego can be very clever at making us think we need all sorts of things that we don't, and these things do nothing but distract us from our innate sense of peace and contentment.

It is this on which so much of our economy is built. Although we're told we live in a capitalistic society, we really live under commercialism. In capitalism, people produce, buy and sell products based on supply and demand. The demand part of the equation is supposed to be about need.

Under commercialism, the same equation is used, but consumers are made to think they need things that they really don't. This causes them to work harder, spend more and earn less. This dynamic not only serves large corporations, but it also serves our egos.

The ego loves to keep us looking for peace in places where we will not find it. As long as you believe you can find peace in a faster car or a better stereo system, you will continue to look for peace but never find it. When you do this, you're damning yourself to a life of wandering in the dark, feeling around for something that is not there.

A more modern approach to tapas would be to take a real inventory of our possessions. Most of us, if we were really honest, would be able to take several truckloads of stuff to Good Will and not miss a thing. I'm not suggesting that we live in poverty and eat only rice. But it is helpful beyond measure to look at our stuff and get rid of what no longer serves us.

George Carlin had a famous comedy routine called "A Place for My Stuff." In it, he went through a very funny monologue on how to manage our stuff. By the end of his routine, it's clear how much energy goes into organizing and protecting and storing our possessions.

This is why we practice tapas. The immense energy that goes into keeping track of our stuff and storing it, not to mention the constant search for more stuff, is one of our greatest distractions in life. By letting go of some of that stress, we find we have more time for the things in life that really matter.

When I lead retreats to developing countries, my students are often struck by how happy the local people can be. They work hard and don't seem to have much, but they smile and they are friendly. Their children may not have shoes or all their vaccinations, but they seem much happier than children in more developed countries. People in these countries work so they can enjoy life and each other's company, rather than working insane hours just to buy more stuff that fails to bring happiness.

As we begin to develop a tapas practice for ourselves, our chief concern, as with all the yamas and niyamas, is mindfulness. In this context, mindfulness means looking at each thing we buy, and all the things we own, and really exploring why each is a 'need' for us. Even if we still buy the product or continue to hold onto it, we will at least have an understanding that it will not bring happiness, and we will be that much closer to searching within.

SVADHYAYA (STUDY)

"Self-study deepens one's communion with one's personal deity."
—YOGA SUTRA 2:44

The fourth niyama is called svadhyaya and it is the practice of study. This niyama has two basic parts—Self-study and the study of scripture. Although I'll describe each aspect of this practice separately, at their pinnacle they become one. Self-study is the practice of exploring one's Self from the inside out, and getting to know that Self on every level. Scriptural study is like looking into a mirror, because the job of any great scripture is to reflect back to the reader that which is within. Both aspects of this practice ultimately give the urban mystic insight into his or her essential nature as Atman.

Self-study is the practice of looking at yourself, which can be a daunting task. Looking at yourself means looking at your inner beauty, as well as the not so attractive parts of the psyche. Within all of us there is incredible light and an unimaginable capacity for love, but we also have a shadow side that can be very overwhelming.

Getting in touch with this shadow side allows us to process it and, when appropriate, express it in a way that is healthy and well adjusted.

Most spiritual traditions, yoga included, begin with what is called a spiritual rebirth of sorts. Many people live good lives and even attend religious services on a regular basis, but something happens to people when they completely surrender to Spirit. This can happen for all sorts of reasons, but is usually characterized by a breakdown of some sort.

This breakdown may be emotional, mental or physical. It can even be economic or social. Whatever the nature of the breakdown, a chain reaction starts.

It's like a match. That match can lie quiet for many years carrying within it the potential for a flame, but nothing happens. When the match is rubbed sufficiently hard against a rough surface, it ignites. Once this process of igniting happens, there is no turning back. There is a brilliant beginning, which is followed by a more stable flame.

Our own awakening happens in much the same way. All of us are in a state of divine potential. In time, when the roughness of the lives that we have created for ourselves rubs sufficiently hard against us, we burst into a brilliant flame.

When this inner flame bursts forth, it carries with it a mandate for change. It's like a prayer carried from the deepest part of the heart and mind that screams, "Show me who I am!" When this happens, what we're really doing is asking the Sadguru to turn our awareness to all the things we hold within that prevent us from seeing our true nature.

It is at this point that a "Fasten Your Seat Belt" sign would be most helpful. The great teacher has just been waiting for the invitation. Now She will show you everything. This process can be very painful and quite unnerving. It can make a person want to return to that latent state where things were quiet but there was no flame. Like the match, there is no going back. Once this process has begun, we will look within. The only question is how painful will the process be. As the old cliché goes, "Sometimes God gets your attention with a gentle tap on the back; other times He uses a baseball bat."

Practicing svadhyaya is the way we make this process gentler. This is not to imply that it will be easy, but the Sadguru will not have to work so hard to get our attention if we meet Her consciously. As we take bold steps along our spiritual path, one of our greatest assets is to open our eyes wide and look at all that is within. In doing this, these blocks can be made fully conscious and can then be set free.

The urban mystic has great tools available to help him or her with this process—things like psychotherapy, spiritual counseling, support groups; even a well-rounded hatha yoga practice can make the practice of opening ourselves up to this Self exploration more fluid. The key to this process is in the willingness.

Without willingness the road will be quite rocky. I have had so many students approach me and ask why their life was thrown into turmoil shortly after they started their yoga practice. I have to explain that when we make the conscious or unconscious commitment to become more peaceful, the universe rearranges itself to show us all the things that are blocking our peace.

Negative Rxn:

In the past year a lot of friends have lost their jobs due to the slowing economy. It's always interesting to note how people deal with things such as the loss of a job. One of my friends, Jacob, was let go because the dotcom where he was working closed its doors. He had been living way outside his means and had counted on stock options to pay for his very expensive lifestyle. In a matter of a few weeks, he had lost his job and his stock options were worthless. The last time I saw him he was on a rather severe drinking and drug binge.

2 Diff. ways of handling bad things

Positive Rxn:

A second friend, Ted, had also run into some hard times with his work. The database company he worked for was downsizing considerably, and he too was given his pink slip. At the same time, the stock market deflated and he was left with a large mortgage and no way of paying it. He decided to take his misfortune and turn it into a blessing. He spent a week at a natural hot spring in Northern

California, and did lots of yoga and personal reflection while he was there. By the end of the week he had not only made peace with his situation, he had decided to follow his dream of living in Africa and helping with the AIDS crisis there. Within two months he had sold his home and was on his way there.

Ted and Jacob are both practicing svadhyaya whether they know it or not. Jacob will no doubt learn something from his experience, though it may be a long time before he figures out exactly what the message is, and there may be some significant suffering along the way. Ted will also have a difficult time ahead, but he will flourish much more quickly, because he is exploring who he is and being proactive about whom he wants to become. Although Ted's practice of svadhyaya may be difficult, the fact that he is walking into life with his eyes open will make the process run so much more smoothly.

Studying sacred texts is the other way to practice svadhyaya. There are many texts that qualify as sacred. India alone has given us dozens, such as the Upanishads, the Vedas and the Yoga Sutra. Other cultures have given us such texts as well. Certainly writings such as The Torah, the Gospels and the Koran fall into this category.

abt the interpretation you need!

The interesting thing about any sacred text is that it mirrors back to the reader that which is within him or her. For example, two people can read the same passage from the Bible. One can see justification for hatred, and the other can find the incentive to forgive. This is why there can be many factions within a single religion such as Christianity.

When we learn to read these texts as mirrors rather than as absolute truth, they grow with us and point to aspects of our being that need to be examined. They are fluid, like a river. Although you can get into the river many times, the water is always changing. Trying to read these texts rigidly is like building a dam in the river and will only create a stagnant swamp.

Early in my yoga practice I picked up the Bhagavad Gita. It is one of the standard texts for yogis to read. As far as books go, it isn't long, so I figured it couldn't be that hard. I had hoped to get through it in one sitting. Prior to reading it, I had expected to open the book and be filled with all sorts of peaceful thoughts and nice feelings. What I found, however, was quite different. It opens with Arjuna, a great warrior, sitting in the middle of a large battlefield. He sees his opponents on all sides and recognizes them as his brothers and kinsmen. This throws him into great despair and he drops his weapon and refuses to fight.

Up until this point, the story seemed to have all the trappings of a Hollywood action film. Arjuna's refusal to fight seemed spiritual enough; after all, most spiritual leaders teach nonviolence. But then the story took an unexpected turn. Krishna appears as Arjuna's chariot driver and agrees to counsel Arjuna. Arjuna explains his situation and collapses in a useless ball of self-pity. Krishna then tells Arjuna to get up and fight. He tells him that not to fight would be dishonorable, and that it is his duty as a warrior to go into this battle. My brain screeched to a halt. This didn't seem much different than a God who would flood the earth, or turn a woman into a pillar of salt. I snapped the book shut and for about a year didn't pick it up again.

What I failed to realize at the time was that it was me who was at war within my own mind, and it was me who was wimping out of the war in a ball of self-pity. At that time I was trying to live my life in a peaceful way, but I was only going through the motions. Smiling and bowing to people and trying to look enlightened was what I thought was required. What I was really doing was backing down from the fight and refusing to heal my own conflicted mind.

As time passed I realized that Arjuna and I had a lot in common. We were both in a war that we didn't want to be in, and we were both conflicted about our loyalties. Neither of us wanted to fight the war, and surrendering would only invite personal destruction. There seemed to be no way out. What really offended me in the Bhagavad Gita was not the fact that it was about war, but rather that it reflected back to my own state of turmoil.

When I did pick up the book again, I was in a very different space. Now I saw Arjuna's despair, but I also saw Krishna offering something fresh and new as a way out. Krishna was teaching Arjuna to fight in a new way by teaching him the path of yoga. *perception can be first of the same thing @ 2 diff points in LIFE!*

The words of the Bhagavad Gita have not changed for thousands of years, but they changed and grew for me. One of the tests that a sacred text must pass is that it grows with its student. It's not something you can ever outgrow. It simply meets you where you are and reflects back to you that which you most need to see in that moment.

Svadhyaya is a powerful and essential part of any yoga practice. It gives us the tools we need to dig deep into the mind and body and to release any blockages we find there. It is this niyama that brings to the surface many of the issues we will confront in the latter six limbs.

– ISHVARA PRANIDHANA (SURRENDER) –

"Through orientation toward the ideal of pure awareness, one can achieve integration."
—YOGA SUTRA 2:45

The fifth niyama is ishvara pranidhana. It literally translates, "Surrender to the Lord." Initially, coming out of my strict Christian background, I didn't have much use for this niyama. I felt as though the Lord of my childhood had abandoned me and I was quite hesitant to surrender to another God who would likely do the same thing.

In time I have grown to embrace this niyama as much as all the others— perhaps even more. It has been a long journey for me, and I struggle with it even today. Yet in spite of all the challenges I have encountered around this niyama, I have to say that it has given me the most in terms of peace of mind and clarity of purpose.

I know I am not alone in my discomfort around ishvara pranidhana. Many people come to yoga because they want to live a more spiritual life. Yoga looks so different from the religion of their childhood, which has often left an unsavory aftertaste. Yoga is a somewhat unique spiritual path because it doesn't ask you to believe anything. While most religions ask you to believe in certain stories or events, such as the parting of the Red Sea or the virgin birth of Jesus, yoga only asks you to have an open mind. In fact, the practice of yoga seems to scream out, "Prove me wrong!"

Yoga doesn't deny that miraculous events, such as those found in the Bible, are possible. In fact, there are countless stories about yogis doing seemingly impossible things, such as levitating. However, believing these stories to be true or historically accurate is not relevant to the effectiveness of your yoga practice.

I believe this is why yoga appeals to so many people who have abandoned the church of their past only to find that there is a spiritual void in their lives. On one hand they don't want to go back to a religion that was in some way abusive, and on the other they feel a strong desire to explore their spiritual nature.

Because so many people come to yoga out of a negative spiritual past, many teachers avoid speaking about this niyama altogether. This is understandable. There is no point in scaring people off. Yet surrender is an important aspect of yoga. Yoga asks us to look at our blocks, not to avoid them and sweep them under the rug. Therefore, when a student of yoga is ready, exploring ishvara pranidhana can be a major step in the healing of one's past.

Ishvara is one of the Hindu gods who shows up from time to time in Hindu mythology. While some students implement this niyama by cultivating a direct relationship with Ishvara, most take a more generic approach. There are people from every religion in the world who have integrated their deeply held religious beliefs with the practice of yoga. It is the loose wording of this niyama in the Yoga Sutra that makes this possible.

When people start to explore this niyama, I think it happens in three basic phases. First, a student must open his or her mind to the possibility that there is a great force in the universe that is organizing and guiding the flow of things. This force can be called by many names, but it is hard to deny that there is some sort of order and meaning around us. For people who come to yoga with a belief in some sort of God or higher power, this step has already been taken.

The next phase is to recognize that this universal wisdom can manage not only the operations of a whole universe, but also can handle the details of our lives. Logic would point out that if you accept the basic idea that the universe has order and is being guided by some type of wisdom, and we are an inseparable part of that universe, then that same force must also guide our lives.

The ego doesn't like this line of logic much. If we were to accept the idea that there is a great and wise force guiding our lives, then we would no longer need the ego to micromanage everything. This is why the ego loves to point to all the starving children and homeless people and try to pin the blame on God.

It's in the third phase that the practice of ishvara pranidhana really becomes a challenge. Accepting the notion that there's a great force guiding the universe is one thing; it's quite another to accept the idea that because we are part of that universe we, too, are guided. Unfortunately, it seems rather too radical an idea that we should trust enough to actually surrender our lives to this force. See if following this logic will help explain the concept:

1.   The Universe is guided by a great intelligence (Spirit).
2.   Because we're part of the Universe, we, too, are guided in the same way.
3.   Therefore, it is logical to allow Spirit to guide our lives.

None of us worry about the sun coming up each day, or that the tides will somehow stop their ebb and flow between low and high. We never question that animals seem to know that in the spring it is time to mate, or that billions of tiny sperm find their way to a tiny egg in the nether regions of a woman's fallopian tubes. Life happens with a perfection and a grace that must inspire awe when we take the time to look at it. Yet in our own lives, most of us cannot seem to trust this force enough to allow it to take the reins.

Ishvara pranidhana is the practice of noticing when we are trying to micromanage our own lives, and then returning the control to Spirit. As I have stated over and over again in this chapter, the niyamas are designed to make room in our lives for the rest of our yoga practice. Nowhere is this more evident than with ishvara pranidhana.

When I started writing my first book, Spiritual Journeys along the Yellow Brick Road, many people put a negative spin on the publishing process. It seemed that everyone I spoke with wanted to affirm that getting published was about as easy as sticking your elbow in your ear. At times I would fall into this negative thinking, but I tried to keep a positive attitude. I kept returning to the idea that my job was to write the book, and if I was the only one to read it, then that was fine. I decided to let Spirit handle the details.

As I would meditate and write, I felt that Spirit was guiding me to do it. It felt natural and good, and I was growing from the experience.

Although I had not even tried to get the book published yet, I decided to put some of what I had written on my website. I figured it was a way of sharing my ideas with the world even if not with the mass market.

Thierry, the owner of Findhorn Press, saw my website and liked what he read. He asked me to write a proposal for the book so he and his wife Karin could consider it for publication. At first, I thought it was a scam, but he answered all my questions and offered me a great contract for a first-time author. I signed the contract with them, and we've had a great relationship ever since.

Now this story has a happy ending. I got published, which was what I had hoped for. But I did so by surrendering the process to Spirit. I was willing to trust Spirit and write the book, even if it never made it into print. As in so many other instances in my life, Spirit not only came through, but also arranged a situation that was far better balanced than anything I could have put together on my own.

Practicing ishvara pranidhana doesn't mean you lie around like a limp noodle waiting for Spirit to do everything. It's about surrendering the ego will and allowing it to be replaced by the will of Spirit. In doing this, we remain fully active in the world, but our efforts are organized and harmonious, and they work in concert with the rest of Spirit's symphony. When we really practice ishvara pranidhana we stop trying to swim upstream, and instead allow the current of life to carry us along without effort or strain.

CHAPTER SEVEN

ASANA
Pose

"These are the indicators of success in [hatha yoga]: leanness of body, clearness of face, distinctness of [voice], very clear eyes, health, [understanding of OM], lighting of the digestive fire, and purity of the nadis."

—HATHA YOGA PRADIPIKA 2:78

TAKING YOUR SEAT

"[Asana] occurs as all effort relaxes and coalescence arises, revealing that the body and the infinite universe are indivisible."

—YOGA SUTRA 2:47

Most people start their yoga practice by doing hatha yoga, the style of yoga that is characterized by poses and breathing. Hatha yoga is based on the eight limbs that Patanjali outlined in his Yoga Sutra, but it focuses a significant amount of its attention on the third limb or asana.

The word asana literally means 'sit', but modern yogis usually translate it as 'pose.' Although the sacred text says little about yoga poses, they are what yoga is best known for here in the West.

In our fast paced world, what most of us need to do more than anything else is to 'sit.' We rush from activity to activity and never quiet down long enough to realize that we are only rushing to our death. Learning to sit still is paramount if we ever hope to realize our true nature as spiritual beings.

I highly recommend a thorough study of the various poses, but their details are something best learned in a class taught by a qualified teacher. There are also many excellent books that cover poses from the viewpoint of the major hatha yoga traditions. Rather than focus this chapter on the specifics of each pose, I would like to explore some of the poses' spiritual and psychological aspects and discuss some ways in which you can take your poses to a new level.

If hatha yoga were nothing more than an exercise, I don't think it would have survived as long as it has. Indeed, the asanas are associated with profound physical benefits, but they are so much more. When you practice and breathe into them, the poses change you. Sometimes the changes are subtle, but most often they are immediate and tangible.

As I mentioned above, the word asana translates, 'sit.' This is highly significant when we consider the poses because it has a direct effect on the rest of the eight limbs. When you look at the whole of your life, you will probably see a very clear pattern. In every aspect of your life, you have probably tried to avoid the uncomfortable as much as possible. Unfortunately, this pattern, which may seem totally justified, is the root of unmitigated suffering in your life.

Like the humming bird that flits from flower to flower, our egos would have us dart from one thing to the next, like digging a well but moving each time you lift a shovel full of dirt. Rather than a deep hole that yields water, you wind up with a yard that resembles Swiss cheese. When we practice asana, we sit, or hold the poses on the yoga mat of life. In doing this we are able to go deeper into the experience of life and truly grow and heal.

This is why marriage can be such a powerful tool in relationships. When two people get married, they commit to sticking in out, no matter what. It would be easy to bail when things heat up, but in marriage you commit to sitting it out and working through difficulties to gain the freedom those challenges obscure. When you sit rather than walking away, growth happens.

The same is true for everything in life. By learning to practice asana, by learning to sit with the discomfort you find in various yoga poses, you learn to do the same in life. That's why asana, whether practiced in a flowing sequence or in a more gentle restorative way, frequently has a profound and transformative effect that reaches far beyond the yoga mat.

When I first started taking yoga, a woman who had a perfect body was frequently in class. She could bend her body into all sorts of shapes with ease and she never seemed to struggle. I remember thinking, "Wow, she must be so evolved." But as I got to know her a bit more, I realized that she was emotionally unstable and not very nice. While she was flexible in her body, the more important aspects of her life were in shambles.

Therefore, I feel it's important to note one thing before moving forward. Although enlightenment and inner peace are the natural result of doing yoga, it's important to realize that just because a person can contort his or her body into a number of complex and difficult poses, doesn't mean he or she is more spiritual. Likewise, if a person has difficulty executing even the basic poses, this doesn't make that person less spiritual.

It's the practice of moving into, holding, and releasing from the various poses that clears the mind and trains us to respond to life in a more centered fashion. Therefore, try not to focus on how well you do the poses, but rather on the fact that you keep returning to your practice. That's all you need to do.

───── ASANA AS A METAPHOR ─────

"[Asanas] give steadiness, health and lightness of body."
—HATHA YOGA PRADIPIKA 1:17

Last fall I led my annual yoga retreat to Joshua Tree National Park in southern California. (www.desertspritretreat.com) One of the participants, Peter, had been married to his high school sweetheart for nearly twenty years. They had several children together, the youngest of whom had gone off to college just two months before.

His marriage was not violent or abusive, but he was no longer in love. His wife had confessed to having had an affair several years earlier, yet he hadn't sought a divorce. Even though he stayed in the relationship, he had stopped trusting her. He held onto their frail marriage out of fear. One afternoon, while sitting on one of the giant boulders near our campsite, Peter spoke with me about his marriage, "I don't know if it's the fear of being alone, or the fear of trying to find a new partner," he said. "I just feel like I'm going to fall apart every time I think about leaving her. I don't trust her or love her any more, but the thought of being alone feels like someone's kicking my legs out from under me."

Several days later, during one of our afternoon practices, Peter felt something shift. He was holding the warrior pose, and struggling very much with it. It had never been an easy pose for him, and he usually left the pose before the rest of the group. On this day, however, he stayed with it. He deepened his breath and allowed his body to shake and tremble. He later told me, "I was afraid of the intense sensations that were coming up; I felt like I was going to throw up, but I was tired of this pose ruining my yoga practice. I wanted to know what it was like to come to a class and not be thinking about the dreaded warrior pose before I even had my shoes off."

"I stuck it out, and I did it. I thought I would die, but I didn't. I couldn't stop smiling through the rest of the class. When I was in deep relaxation, I decided that I want to do this with everything in my life. And I'm going to start with my marriage."

Peter went home and spoke with his wife. He had intended to ask her for a divorce, but when they got to talking, they decided to try to make a go of things. They started going to couples counseling and eventually started taking yoga together. The last time I spoke with Peter, he and his wife were going to a couple's retreat at the Kripalu Yoga Center in Massachusetts.

While Peter's marriage may be unique, his experience with yoga is not. Many people come to yoga to heal a bad back or to gain more flexibility, but quickly realize that what has changed is their whole way of dealing with life. They find that the entirety of their lives is changed by the seemingly unrelated practice of yoga poses and breathing.

Our minds are very habit oriented. Your mental response to the events in our life doesn't change much. As much as we'd like to think that in each situation our reactions are unique, they are only reactions. External circumstances will change, but our minds tend to run the same recording over and over, making only the slightest changes to fit a given circumstance.

When we enter into a yoga pose, we intentionally put ourselves in an uncomfortable position. We then have a choice. We can respond to the pose in the same way we respond to every other uncomfortable situation in life, or we can apply the principles of yoga to it.

For example, take triangle pose (trikonasana). Most people find the pose at least a bit challenging, and some find it extremely difficult. In either case, you can come into the pose and notice your mind start to churn— thinking about the next pose, or calling this pose all sorts of names. You may even start to compare your pose to those of other people in the room. There are a whole variety of things your mind can do.

Then you hear the teacher reminding you to breathe deeply into the pose. As you do this, you find the drama of the mind begin to quiet. Perhaps it won't shut down completely but it will settle down a bit. Gradually you find that the pose becomes less painful. The same amount of physical sensation is there, but the suffering that the mind creates has been lessened.

In addition, you can now look at the pose from a more centered place. You can start to explore the pose and notice ways to deepen or modify it. Many times when we are in a pose, the mind's chatter hides the important messages that the body is trying to tell us. By breathing into the pose we can hear these messages and act accordingly.

When I lived in Providence, Rhode Island, I was part of a meditation group. We were all very close and came together for many reasons that in the beginning were unclear. One of the members of the group was a man named Jimmy who was wise way beyond his twenty-three years. Jimmy had been practicing yoga and meditation for several years when I met him. He had a great sense of humor and was more committed to meditation than just about anyone I had ever met. He had a strong incentive. There was a rare tumor developing in his spine, and nothing seemed to help. As it grew, it would move up his spinal cord, putting pressure on various nerves and causing pain and paralysis. He was told that eventually this tumor would take his life.

He fought however, and did everything he could to keep his body strong and his mind sharp. After one of our groups, I mentioned an article that I had just read about figs. According to this article, some scientists in Japan were using an extract from figs to treat various tumors and were having some success. Jimmy smiled. It turned out that he had been craving figs for weeks. His mother had been buying bags of them but couldn't seem to keep enough in the house. His body had known what it needed, and Jimmy was able to keep his mind quiet enough to listen.

Our asana practice teaches us to do the same thing. Life is like a sticky mat; each circumstance in which we find ourselves is like a pose. Some poses are hard to hold; others are pleasant. But it is how we hold the pose that determines whether or not we will suffer or grow, and whether or not we will listen to the drama of the ego or the wisdom of our Spirit.

In my talks, I frequently use the example of sitting in traffic. There are few experiences in our modern world that can push me into insanity like a traffic jam. As my yoga practice deepened, I noticed that my reactions in traffic were much more centered, not to mention, more polite.

There was a time when I would use my middle finger at least as much as the clutch while I was driving. Now I have turned traffic into a conscious practice. As my body and mind become uncomfortable, I deepen my breath and smile. Sometimes I'll even turn off the radio and chant for a while, or repeat my mantra silently to myself. This does not change the external circumstances; I still sit in traffic until it starts to move, but my body and mind are at peace.

This same principle works for all of life's poses. Try it the next time you're having trouble with a boss or family member, or the next time you're butting heads with your romantic partner. Breathe and relax. Acknowledge that it may be uncomfortable, but try not to engage your mind in the drama. Be open to the possibility that you could hold this uncomfortable pose, be at peace, and learn something.

This is why working with yoga poses on the yoga mat is a practice. The work we do on the yoga mat is the rehearsal. The work we do on the mat of life is the great performance. And when we give a command performance, life seems to give us everything we need to find the peace we're longing for.

―――――― **ASANA AND EVOLUTION** ――――――

"Those who aspire to the state of yoga should seek the Self in inner solitude through meditation. With the body and mind controlled they should constantly practice one-pointedness, free from expectations and attachments to material possessions."
―BHAGAVAD GITA, CHAPTER 6:10

Spiritual evolution is what living the contemplative life is all about. Whether you practice yoga or some other form of mysticism, the ultimate purpose is the evolution of consciousness. The practice of yoga is deeply concerned with our spiritual evolution because through it we find liberation from our suffering.

In his best selling book, The Road Less Traveled, M. Scott Peck had this to say about spiritual evolution:

Again and again I have emphasized that the process of spiritual growth is an effortful and difficult one. This is because it is conducted against a natural resistance, against a natural inclination to keep things the way they were, to cling to the old maps and old ways of doing things, to take the easy path.... As in the case of physical evolution, the miracle is that this resistance is overcome. We do grow. Despite all that resists the process, we do become better human beings. Not all of us. Not easily. But in significant numbers humans somehow manage to improve themselves and their cultures. There is a force that somehow pushes us to choose the more difficult path whereby we can transcend the mire and muck into which we are so often born.

This is one of the key reasons why we develop an asana practice. Our natural inclination is to take the easy path. When we enter into a pose, there is a natural resistance to it. Let's face it, most yoga poses are not the most comfortable. We find ourselves twisted into some pretty odd shapes. When we find a great deal of resistance to the poses, it's tempting to want to check out and let the mind wander. And yet, when we step forward and keep breathing into the pose, we find liberation from the fear that once held us back.

It takes tremendous courage to move past the edge of our comfort and step boldly to the edge of what we know and feel comfortable with. Evolution happens when we move beyond our comfort level and explore new territory.

Can you imagine how courageous it must have been for that first fish to hop out of the ocean onto dry land? Of course evolution didn't happen quite that quickly, but there is a nice analogy here. Making that leap from familiar surroundings in the ocean to the complete unknown of dry land is bad enough, but it is doubtful that any of the other fish lent much support, which is perhaps worse.

This is what our lives are like in so many ways. The old way doesn't work, but the new way is completely unknown. So we can sit and suffer, or we can take that step onto dry land. We can listen to the naysayers in our lives, or we can trust that tiny voice that says, "Jump—I'll catch you and lift you to higher ground."

Several years ago, a woman named Janet came into my class. She had just completed my Introduction to Yoga Workshop, and was getting started in this new way of life. As we practiced, I could see the difficulty she was having with the poses. In the beginning, most find the practice difficult, but Janet seemed to find it especially trying.

She rested in child pose (balasana) through much of the practice, and when doing other poses, she had a pained expression on her face. I knew yoga would be good for her, but wasn't sure if she would stick it out. I intended to check in with her after class, but she left in a hurry and I didn't have a chance. I thought for sure she had had a terrible time and that I would never see her again.

Janet surprised me, however, and continued. She struggled for the first few months of her practice, but in time things seemed to get a bit easier for her. However, there were always a few poses that she would avoid. One was the upward facing bow (urdhva dhanurasana). During each class, when it came time to do this pose, she would just sit and watch everyone else, not even giving it a shot. Just watching others do the pose seemed to bring up fear.

Then, one day when I least expected it, she called me over and asked me if I could help her. I could see that she was very nervous and didn't think she could do it, but she had a willingness to try.

I showed her how to use the wall and a few blocks to support the pose and make pushing up a bit easier. She struggled and almost gave up, but I reminded her to breathe and put my hands under her shoulders for added support. She pushed up and lifted her head several inches off the floor and then slowly lowered down.

I don't think I have ever seen someone so happy or so empowered. She was glowing. She may not have done the pose perfectly, but she did break through that fear. For the longest time she was like that fish that swam around the edge, wanting to leap out into a new level but afraid to do so. On that day, she did it.

This, of course, translates into life. There are so many areas of our life where we feel stuck and paralyzed by fear. The old way has got to go, but the new way is too fearful and unknown. Asana teaches us that this is natural and shows us how to make that leap.

There was a time when a woman's right to vote was thought a radical notion, and the idea of slavery was accepted by most. The people who led the march toward change were a lot like Janet. I can't imagine that Abraham Lincoln looked forward to the difficult time that he knew would follow on the signing of the Emancipation Proclamation, and I can't believe that Lucy Stone, relished the idea of being called names and regarded as anti-feminine by many women of her day. Janet, Abraham Lincoln, and Lucy Stone saw something that needed to be done and, when the time was right, they pushed through their fears and did it.

Our asana practice is the trial run. If you can work through your fear of the handstand, then it will be that much easier to find the courage to leave your secure job for the occupation that will be really satisfying. This is how we prepare for evolution.

——— BRAHMA, VISHNU AND SHIVA ———

"You are the creator and destroyer and our protector. You shine as the sun in the sky; you are the source of all light."
—PRASHNA UPANISHAD 2:9

According to Hindu mythology, 'God' is believed to be a Trinity. Like the Christian Trinity which describes God as the Father, Son and Holy Spirit, the Hindu Trinity involves three parts that are really One, and yet seem to be separate.

From a Hindu perspective the three aspects of God are Brahma, Vishnu and Shiva. There are many other gods in Hindu mythology, but these are the three primary godheads. All the others fall under one of these three.

Brahma is the creator who brought the whole universe into being and is constantly creating. We can see Brahma at work in the blooming of a flower and in the birth of a child. Brahma is the impetus for all of life.

Vishnu is the aspect of God that sustains life. He is the harvest and the sunlight. He is the aspect of our being that provides us with all we need to learn our lessons so that we can grow and evolve in this physical universe. He is the air that fills our lungs and the food that fills our bellies. Without Vishnu life could not exist.

Shiva is the aspect of God that transforms. He is often thought of as the destroyer because he breaks down the old, allowing things to be reborn in the next cycle. Shiva is often feared because he's associated with death, but if it were not for Shiva, birth could not happen.

You've probably seen depictions of these gods. They frequently have many arms and legs and are adorned with a variety of symbols. This can put some people off because they see the myth as being false and outdated in this age of science. However, the Truth that inspired the myth is very real, for in all of life we can see these three forces as they dance together.

In our human life we are created at birth, live, and then die. Our planet has seasons of birth, life and death. Even the cells of our body are continuously being created, living and then dying. All of life follows this dance. It's the most natural thing there is, and yet we resist this flow more often than we realize.

In order to feel truly happy in this world, we must learn to appreciate all aspects of our existence and see how they all work together. Brahma, Vishnu and Shiva must work together in our lives, or we will find a lack of balance. Disease is the natural result of this lack of harmony.

Learning to balance these three forces isn't easy. We're taught to fear the death that Shiva brings, and not to trust Vishnu's abundance. It's even easy to fear the new and unexplored territory into which we are urged by Brahma's wild creativity. It's our egos that doubt and do not trust, and that's what leads to fear and suffering. Learning to let Brahma, Vishnu and Shiva dance freely in our lives is an essential part of living as an urban mystic. A mindful asana practice can really help with this because each pose is designed to mimic the natural dance of Brahma, Vishnu and Shiva. By working through the poses in a conscious way, we prepare ourselves to live more fully balanced lives.

When we start each pose, there is a period of creation. In this stage of the pose we find our alignment and focus on the details of the pose. This alignment is what gives the pose form and distinguishes it from the other poses. This is also where we create a pose that is safe and nonthreatening to our physical body. When we ignore or brush over Brahma working in this part of the pose, injury is the likely result. But when we allow the pose to be created in our bodies in a mindful and conscious way, we open the energy pathways and prepare our minds to sit in the pose.

I remember once, about a year into my yoga practice, going into kapotasana, the pigeon pose, one I had done many times before, when my teacher, Ellie, came and pressed one of my hips gently down and forward. I felt the pose reach deeply into my other hip, releasing a palpable flow of energy up and down my body. It was truly as if I was doing the pose for the first time. The pose was fresh and new, like nothing I had ever felt. This was my body and mind aligning with the force of Brahma.

Once we have aligned our bodies in the pose, we hold. Some styles of yoga will ask you to hold the pose for five breaths and others for fifteen minutes or more. However, the length of time you wind up holding the pose is not as important as surrendering into it. By quieting the mind and looking at the pose from a natural and quiet place we can experience Vishnu sustaining the pose. This is an amazing experience.

During my experience with the pigeon pose, I felt that release of energy led to a profound perception of support. I could feel the earth beneath me creating a stable foundation, and I could feel Ellie's firm yet compassionate assist pressing me deeper into the pose. I could even feel the breathing of other students in the room reminding me to breathe deeply myself. This was Vishnu at work.

At last we released the pose. It is my observation that most injuries in yoga occur when people are coming out of a pose. They work hard to come into the details and then give everything they have to holding the pose, but when it comes time to let go, they come out mindlessly. By working Shiva into a pose, we leave it with full awareness. We avoid falling out of the pose or releasing like a snapped rubber band. This brings us to an open and mindful place where we can create the next pose.

After Ellie left me to assist the next person, I pushed back into a child pose. My eyes filled with tears. I was not crying out of sadness or even joy. There was a shift in energy, though. It was physical, emotional and mental in nature, and beyond all three. I could feel something let go within me. I was different. It seemed like I was an etch-a-sketch, and some great force had shaken me forcefully yet lovingly, removing a long outdated pattern or design. This was Shiva.

And so goes our asana practice. Over and over again we seek to dance with Brahma, Vishnu and Shiva. This opens our body, heart and mind to new possibilities and new ways of being. This is what many call a paradigm shift, or a shift in consciousness, because old patterns get erased and new pathways are created that are healthier and more evolved.

PSYCHOLOGY AND THE PRACTICE OF ASANA

"They find their joy, their rest, and their light completely within themselves. United with the Lord, they attain nirvana in Brahman."
—BHAGAVAD GITA, CHAPTER 5:24

Several years ago I met a young boy who was very wise. His name was Bodhi, and his mother, Clare, owned a beautiful home just north of the Golden Gate Bridge. I was hoping to rent her home for the weekend to lead a retreat. I was a bit concerned that she had a six-year-old boy, considering that it's hard enough for an adult to sit still for an entire weekend. Clare assured me that Bodhi would not be in the way, and also that our activities would not infringe on his playtime. She had an almost devilish grin when she said this, which led me to believe there was more to this child than she was telling me.

When the weekend of the retreat came, I met Bodhi for the first time. He seemed like a harmless enough child, but I still found it hard to believe that he could contain his youthful energy for a whole weekend. Bodhi was a very special child, however, and I quickly realized there would be no problem. He came up to me, offered his hand and introduced himself. Then he said, "I have a joke. Wanna hear it?"

Expecting a simplistic 'knock-knock' joke, I nodded.

"Why shouldn't you buy a vacuum cleaner from a Buddhist?"

"I don't know. Why?" I said smiling, wondering how, at his age, he even knew what a Buddhist was.

"Because they don't have any attachments!" he said laughing.

I laughed with him, but was amazed that he would even remember a joke like that. He then went on to explain the joke to me. "The Buddha said that when we have attachments, we suffer, so Buddhists don't want to have attachments...not even on their vacuum cleaners." He giggled and ran off to play.

It took me a while to remove my jaw from the floor. Bodhi understood in just six years what I had been trying to grasp for ten of my adult years. His cute little joke reminds us all, in a very simple and innocent way, why we suffer in this world. More importantly, it reminds us of how we can escape from that suffering.

I think it's important to define suffering. Pain is sensation created by the body to warn us of danger or to tell us that something has gone wrong. Frequently we view pain as a bad thing, but really pain is a very good thing, as it helps us to grow and warns us when things are out of balance.

Suffering, on the other hand, is of the mind. It's a story told by the ego that cloaks the truth about who we are. This of course leads to a useless form of discomfort. Rather than inspire growth or warn us of danger, suffering holds us back. It's like a deep pool of mud where your tires are spinning. The more you let them spin in it, the deeper you sink.

Our asana practice helps us look at our attachments and let them go. When we show up in a pose, we most often have expectations about it. Our ego drama has a defined set of stories about each given pose: "This is going to hurt", or "I can't do this well enough," or "I'll be happy when I can do this pose perfectly."

All of these statements are attachments. We can form attachments to both pleasure and pain, and this supports the ego's overall belief in separation. When we surrender into the pose, we poke holes in the ego's story and we start to let go of our attachments. The initial result is a more ecstatic experience on the yoga mat. Of course, it's wonderful to have a great experience on the mat, but the real reward comes when the other psychological attachments in your life also start to fade away. The ego's thinking is held together in a very shabby and haphazard way. When you start to knock over attachments in the asana practice, there's a domino effect, and the rest of your mind starts to become less attached to the way that life unfolds.

This enables us to surrender into the natural flow of life and make our own lives more fulfilling. We still experience pain in our lives, but the suffering begins to drift away, leaving in its wake a quiet mind and an open heart.

Our asana practice heals us psychologically in another way by changing our relationship to the body. As I mentioned in Chapter One, the ego has the belief that we are separate from Spirit and separate from our true nature. In order for the ego to maintain this lie, it needs to find lots of evidence to prove its case. There is no better example of our separation than the body. In a sense, the body is the perfect demonstration of our weakness and insignificance. If you believe you are a body, then you're consenting to the belief that you are your ego, which is the root of all your suffering. Bodies age and get sick. They experience aches and pains and have many limitations. Bodies are confined to time and space and, if all that weren't proof enough, bodies eventually die.

If you believe you are a body, then you believe you're a temporary being that is weak and subject to age, illness and death. Of course, yoga teaches us that we are not the body, but this is a difficult case to make when it feels so real to be in this body. It's hard to say, "The body is an illusion," when your head hurts or your stomach is upset.

This is one of the most powerful aspects of asana. Rather than trying to deny the body and all its aches, pains and limitations, the practice of asana brings us fully into the body. It allows us to transcend the limits of the body by causing us to realize that the body is not who we are.

In the Bible, Saint Paul declares, "The body is the temple of the Spirit." This statement is very much in alignment with the principles of asana. Through asana, we take away the ego's best friend and star witness and we turn it into a vessel through which Spirit can be expressed in this world. The body becomes a temple for us. Where the body was once seen as a dangerous war zone, asana teaches us to see it as sacred space where our Spirit can dwell in peace.

This deflates the ego's case that you are small and insignificant. It's like an old Perry Mason episode where the key witness gets caught in a lie or major contradiction, allowing Perry to win the case by turning the tables and using the opposition's evidence to prove his own point.

I've often seen this happen in people living with HIV. In the beginning, many feel fearful of the virus. It threatens their health and their life. But as they practice hatha yoga, things shift. They begin to realize that life is more than the simple avoidance of sickness and death, and the very virus that once threatened to take their life now becomes the vehicle through which they can access life's beauty. After seeing this process over and over again, I have nicknamed HIV, "The Gift in Ugly Wrapping Paper."

There's a third way the poses can heal us and promote health on a psychological level. Each of the poses is an archetype or a symbol, which speaks to a deep level of the unconscious mind. In other words, the mere act of entering into a pose changes our minds and opens us up on an extremely deep level.

Swami Shri Kripalvanandji, was a great yogi from India and the guru of Yogi Amrit Desai who founded Kripalu Yoga. At the age of nineteen, a series of suicide attempts led him to his guru, who taught him some powerful yoga techniques. Ironically, these techniques did not include the traditional poses associated with hatha yoga. He practiced these techniques for hours each day, and in time became one of the great yogis to come out of India in this century.

One of the most fascinating things about his story is that he would enter into deep states of consciousness through his practice of breathing and meditation, and would oftentimes find himself spontaneously entering into yoga poses and mudras which he had never learned from his guru or any other teacher. These poses seemed to be the natural result of his mind letting go and sinking into a deep state of consciousness.

One of the theories about the origin of some basic yoga poses is that great masters would enter into these deep states of consciousness and find themselves in odd positions. In time, they realized that putting their students into these poses would possibly have the effect of helping them reach the same deep states of awareness. This, of course, turned out to be the case.

Try this basic experiment:

- Sit upright, lift the chest slightly and drop the shoulders away from the ears.
- Notice how you feel.
- Now hunch over a bit, rolling the shoulders forward and caving the chest in a bit.
- Again, notice how you feel.

Most often, we feel uplifted and present when we sit upright, and when we slouch, we tend to find ourselves feeling more depressed and lethargic. Who would have guessed that your second grade teacher was a closet yogi and knew what she was talking about when she told you to sit up straight!

This is a simple example of how our mind and mood are affected by the way we hold our body. Each of the hatha poses works the mind in very powerful ways. Similar to the Native American Medicine Animals that work to open the mind at a level not easily accessed by our conscious mind, each pose works to release old patterns—patterns that are buried deeply within the unconscious mind and that mold our lives in ways which seem beyond our control. As we enter into the poses, they help us to release these deeply held patterns. This moves us into a heightened state of awareness, and shifts at the deepest levels of the mind become a more conscious choice.

Take, for instance, the fish pose (matsyasana). To do this pose you lie on your back and arch your spine upward, lifting your heart toward the sky. Like all of the poses, there are many physical benefits associated with the fish, such as increased immune functioning and a more balanced metabolism. And on a psychological level the fish pose opens the heart and helps us replace bitterness and resentment with compassion and love.

At the end of a class one of my students, Lance, was doing the fish when he started to cry. The tears were soft at first and then fell harder and harder. He continued to cry quietly through deep relaxation as well. When the class finished, I spoke with him, and he told me about his experience. About a year earlier, he and his boyfriend had broken up. He had worked consciously through a lot of his resentment and anger, but on an unconscious level he was still unable to forgive his ex-lover for leaving him. During his experience with the fish pose, he became aware of these hidden feelings and was able to breathe through them. By the time deep relaxation came around, he had moved from anger to compassion for his former partner.

Of course, a major emotional release that ends in compassion won't happen every time a person does the fish or any other pose. But the poses do open us to levels we are often unable to access consciously. This is why hatha yoga works so well in conjunction with psychotherapy and/or spiritual counseling.

By putting ourselves into the asanas and breathing into them, we begin to work on that level of the unconscious mind which great masters such as Swami Shri Kripalvanandji worked on consciously. This allows us to clear our samskaras, or mental and energetic impurities, and move to a more complete expression of our true Self, which is what the practice of yoga is all about.

CHAPTER EIGHT

PRANAYAMA the Breath of Life

---

*"Man and woman, beast and bird live by breath.
Breath therefore is called the true sign of life."*
—TAITTIRIYA UPANISHAD 2:3.1

---

*"Just as the lion, tiger and elephant is tamed step by step,
so is the breath controlled."*
—HATHA YOGA PRADIPIKA 2:15

When I teach my Introduction to Yoga workshop, the first topic I cover is how to breathe. It's the most essential part of hatha yoga, and the gateway into the higher limbs that we will be covering in upcoming chapters. When we do yoga poses without conscious breathing, they are little more than stretches. The stretches themselves have benefits, but their true potential cannot be fully realized without the breath. When we combine the asanas (poses) with deep, mindful breathing, they become a powerful tool for cutting through our mental, physical and emotional blocks.

Pranayama is the fourth limb of yoga that Patanjali outlined in his Yoga Sutra. There are many pranayama techniques that can be practiced, ranging from simple to very advanced, but they all have a similar effect on our psychology and our sense of Self. These breathing techniques are the doorway into a heightened sense of awareness and a deeper sense of the deep unconscious mind.

The Bible used by Jews and Christians also emphasizes the fundamental principle of breath, for when God created Adam, He breathed the "breath of life" into his lungs. Interestingly, the Hebrew word for 'Spirit' and for 'breath' is the same— "neshamah"

Although breathing seems simple enough, most have not learned to do it well. I often compare the breath to bread. White bread will fill us up and can easily drive away our hunger pains, but it's not really nourishing. It may keep us alive and help us to survive, but it can't really promote good health. In fact a steady diet of white bread will diminish health and dramatically affect our longevity. Whole wheat bread on the other hand does more than simply convince us that we are full. It provides us with nutrients that help our bodies to heal and grow. White bread may enable us to survive and deaden our hunger pains, but whole wheat bread allows us to thrive.

Most of us have learned to breathe in a white bread sort of way. The breath tends to be shallow and fast. This breath is like white bread in that it will keep us alive and it may even keep us from feeling as if we are suffocating, but that's all it will do. Breathing in this way keeps us in survival mode, and until we change the breath, it will be very hard to grow and evolve, because we will be like a skipping record that repeats the same note over and over.

Pranayama is the practice of breathing in a whole-wheat fashion. When we do this, we not only give the body much needed oxygen, but we also fill our chakras and nadis with prana. We shift both the mind and body into evolution mode rather than staying stuck in survival, and we create a stable foundation upon which we can move into the higher limbs of yoga.

Let's turn our attention to the breath then, and explore the practice of pranayama. I want to demonstrate how the pranayama works, so in this chapter I'll be focusing on only a few of the basic breathing techniques. The more advanced techniques are best learned from an experienced yoga teacher. Yet even the most basic breathing exercises have a profound effect on our spiritual growth, so be sure to practice them with mindfulness.

—— THE PHYSIOLOGY OF BREATHING ——

"As long as the breath is in the body, there is life. Death is the departure of the breath. Therefore one should restrain the breath."
—HATHA YOGA PRADIPIKA 2:3

Several years ago I took a vacation to the Hawaiian Island of Maui. My goal was to spend as much time as I could on the beach, doing yoga, swimming and getting a tan. I found a great stretch of white sand called Little Makena Beach, and there I parked my beach chair to enjoy the sun and surf.

While I was there I found a new love for snorkeling. Snorkeling at Little Makena Beach made me feel a lot like that little plastic scuba diver you see in fish tanks, because I found myself among numerous colorful fish and exotic coral formations. It almost seemed unreal. One of the most amazing things about snorkeling at this location was the family of giant sea turtles that lived there. At first I didn't know how to respond to these beautiful creatures. They were large and slow, but graceful and free. They seemed so centered and quiet.

As I swam at the surface, breathing through my snorkel, I felt like a casual observer. I was reminded of a documentary I had seen about animals with very long life cycles, and the giant sea turtles were right at the top. According to this documentary, there was a correlation between the rate of respiration and an animal's life expectancy. It seemed that the slower and deeper various animals breathed, the longer they were likely to live.

Dogs, for example, breathe fast and heavy and only live about twelve years. Rabbits and rodents breathe even more frequently and have an even shorter life span, whereas animals like the sea turtles breathe very deep and very slow and can live for over a hundred years. This principle was not lost to ancient yogis who developed advanced techniques for breath regulation based on this very observation. In fact, Paramahansa Yogananda makes this very point in his book Autobiography of a Yogi.

Watching these very old creatures move so fluidly and freely, I was inspired to deepen my breathing through the snorkel. I started practicing dirga pranayama. In this breath, you fill and empty the lungs completely. The breath is intentionally slow and full, allowing the entire capacity of the lungs to be realized. As I did this, the colors of the fish and coral seemed to get more vivid, and my already relaxed experience became even more lucent.

I felt inspired to quit my role as casual observer, and I dove down as deep as I could. I tried not to get too close to the turtles, as I didn't want to disturb them. I came up for air a few times, but after a few dives, I became less and less dependent on the breath. On the third or fourth dive, two of the sea turtles came to investigate, and began to swim with me. They were less than three feet from me, and they seemed to want to play. I reluctantly came up for air, but went down many more times. I spent most of that afternoon playing with these awesome beings. What was amazing was how alive I felt from using my breath in such a deep and conscious way. My body and mind slipped into a state that was so relaxed and peaceful that I felt like time stood still, and I could feel a great rejuvenation that was reminiscent of a childhood nap.

What happened to me that day was something we strive to create each time we practice yoga. It's not something that happens by accident or even something that is difficult to achieve. In fact, it's based in large part on our nervous system and our physiology.

A significant part of the human body is beyond our conscious control. Functions such as the heartbeat, digestion and elimination are under the control of the autonomic nervous system (ANS). The ANS is what keeps track of all the little details, so we can focus on more evolved things. It keeps us from forgetting to breathe, for instance. Without the ANS, we would spend an enormous amount of energy thinking about things that we normally take for granted, such as healing a cut finger and keeping the heart beating.

The ANS has two basic subdivisions known as the sympathetic nervous system and the parasympathetic nervous system. Both of these subdivisions are essential to our survival and our sense of well being, but for very different reasons. When we allow the mind to be quiet, these two limbs of the ANS work in harmony. When we allow our egos to run the show, these two systems fall into a state of imbalance.

The sympathetic nervous system is often called the 'fight or flight' system. It's responsible for dealing with emergencies. For example, if a large, hungry bear were chasing you, the fight or flight aspect of the ANS would tell your adrenal glands to release adrenaline. It would also tell your heart to beat faster and your lungs to breathe more quickly. It would instruct the internal organs to constrict slightly for protection, while simultaneously sending blood from those organs to the arms and legs to help in the getaway.

The parasympathetic nervous system is often called the 'rest and digest' system. It's this branch of the ANS that tells the body how to function when there is no immediate danger. When this system is engaged, the breath is deep and full and the heartbeat is slow and rhythmic. The vital organs are relaxed and have plenty of blood to function at maximum efficiency. It's the parasympathetic nervous system that allows us to eat a healthy meal, digest it fully, assimilate the important nutrients, and then eliminate the unneeded portion. It's this aspect of the ANS that regulates the immune system and governs the kidneys' blood filtering function.

Although both aspects of the ANS are essential, many of us spend far too much time in fight or flight mode even though we don't live in immediate physical danger. The ANS doesn't know the difference between real physical danger and the stress created by the mind. Therefore, when our mind is overactive, our bodies live in a state of 'fight or flight' rather than one of 'rest and digest.' This has dire consequences for our health and well-being.

Because the ANS operates unconsciously, it's very difficult to regulate it. For example, a person's blood pressure may be elevated because of job stress. That person may even be aware of that stress and the need for change, but because the ANS is largely an unconscious part of our wiring, it's not that simple to just say, "Okay body, lower my blood pressure."

Luckily, we have the breath to work with. The breath is the bodily function that is controlled by both the conscious mind and the ANS. It's also an important part of both 'fight or flight' and 'rest and digest.'

Because we can consciously change the breath, it works as a switch that allows us to choose what aspect of our nervous system will dominate our physiology.

Think about the last time you found yourself late for work and stuck in a traffic jam. Most of us habitually respond with a 'fight or flight' response. I know that I can feel my hands gripping the wheel a bit more tightly, and adrenaline beginning to course through my veins. My shoulders begin to tighten and I find that my vocabulary takes a decidedly steep turn downward in the gutter direction. All of this is part of a 'fight or flight' response. As I have mentioned, this part of the ANS is in place to help us when we are in danger. The problem, of course, is that there is no danger. The traffic jam will not improve with your elevated blood pressure, and adrenaline will serve nothing in this scenario except to weaken the immune system and make you feel like a tiger in a cage.

The next time you find yourself in a traffic jam or some other stressful situation, try breathing deeply and slowly, the way you do in yoga class. Notice how quickly your body returns to a more healthy and rested state. By returning control to the 'rest and digest' part of the ANS, you allow your body to find a natural state of health. This natural state of health becomes the foundation on which we can heal the mind and purify our perceptions of ourselves and the world outside.

—— THE PSYCHOLOGY OF BREATHING ——

"When the breath is unsteady, the mind is unsteady. When the breath is steady, the mind is steady and the yogi becomes steady. Therefore one should restrain the breath."
—HATHA YOGA PRADIPIKA 2:2

The interesting thing about using the breath to counter the physical effects of psychological stress is that the signal travels both ways.

While the initial cause of our physical stress was a mental story that was being expressed in the body, we can change our minds by changing our physiology.

Let's take that traffic jam example again. If you were responding to that traffic jam with mental stress that then led to a 'fight or flight' response on a physical level, you could not only change your physiology by deepening the breath, but could also change your mind at the same time. Because the body and mind are hardwired into each other, they cannot exist in a state of contradiction. The body cannot be in a physical state of stress if the mind is at peace, and the mind cannot be in a state of mental stress if the body is in 'rest and digest.' Therefore, we can quite literally change our thought patterns and our psychology by changing our physiology.

At my last Introduction to Yoga workshop, I covered the basic breathing and yoga poses. In that class there was a young woman named Ashley. She seemed quite resistant to the practice and actually declared at the start of the workshop that she was only there because her romantic partner Susan had dragged her along. I didn't expect that she would do much with the practice, and I was even a little surprised that she stuck it out through the whole workshop. To my surprise, however, she asked me for a copy of my schedule at the conclusion of the workshop and took class with me almost every day for a week. She even came a few times on her own without Susan dragging her along. I could tell she was really enjoying her practice in spite of her initial resistance. After about a week and a half of classes, she approached me with a series of questions.

"I know I wasn't very friendly and warm when I first met you," she said. "I felt like I was being dragged to some New Age cult. All I ever hear about is how great yoga is and I wanted to buck the system and hate it just to be different," she said with a wry grin.

"So why have you continued with your practice?" I asked her.

"I don't know," she replied, "but I can feel it changing me, and for the better. It's almost scary though. I feel like my whole way of thinking is being turned upside down. Hell, some guy at the gas station told me I have a nice smile. I haven't heard that since I was about seven. What's happening to me?"

Before I answered her, I asked, "Do you like the change? Or would you rather keep things the way they were?"

"I like the change a lot, but I'm a bit nervous," she said. "I've only been doing this stuff for about a week, and already I feel like a different person. Part of me is afraid that I won't be recognized at my family reunion in July."

It's the same for all of us when we start a yoga practice. The experience of doing the poses in conjunction with the breathing reprograms the computer, so to speak, and everything we experience from that point on is different.

Finding yourself in a yoga pose is not that much different from finding yourself in a traffic jam or in a difficult relationship. When a pose is done properly, there is no danger to the physical body. Yet in spite of this, the mind tends to create drama around the pose. Most of us start judging either the pose, our bodies, the teacher or the person next to us. We often shake and tremble and wonder why we keep coming back to this awkward space.

If this is where your practice ends, you have cheated yourself. The key is to breathe deeply into the pose, shifting the nervous system from the 'flight or fight' mode to the 'rest and digest' mode. This, of course, has immediate physical and mental benefits. As we have already noted, a shift on the physical level has to translate into a shift on the mental level and vice-versa.

This is only the beginning, however. In addition to making yourself more peaceful and healthy in the moment, you're also breaking an old habit. Rather than meeting the challenge with stress and drama on a physical level, you're training your mind to respond to stressful situations in a new way. You've introduced a choice, and you no longer need to react to life in an unhealthy or un-centered way.

Of course you may still choose to react with 'fight or flight,' but you will at least have the option. In the beginning, this choice will be made in a more conscious way. Most often, when you find yourself in the middle of a situation causing you stress, and when you realize your mind and body are no longer at peace, you will breathe deeply and pull the mind back under control. The more you practice pranayama, the more natural this choice for peace will become, and you'll find that you go down the dead end road less and less often.

The last time I moved, I found a box of old journals. I spent a nostalgic hour or so pouring through them. It was interesting to see how my early journals were filled with dramas and stress. In one, I wrote three pages about my anger and frustrations regarding the Gulf War. I could see the tension in my writing, and I remembered being so passionate about the way our government was handling the whole situation.

Today, I'm still very politically aware, and I love a good protest, but I no longer let the events of the world rob me of my peace of mind. I see the problems that face our world; I try to be a part of the solution, but I no longer respond with anger. At first I thought that taking a more peaceful approach to life would mean letting go of the idea of being proactive, but I've learned that I can be much more effective when I maintain my center.

Because of my pranayama practice, my mind responds differently than it once did. It happened so naturally and smoothly that I hardly noticed.

- PRANAYAMA AND THE ENERGY BODY -

"Like milk and water blended together, mind and breath have the same action. Where there is breath, there is thinking. Where there is mind, there is breathing."
—HATHA YOGA PRADIPIKA 4:24

Just the physical and psychological effects of pranayama make it an invaluable practice, but those benefits pale in comparison with the energetic effects of a strong pranayama practice. In fact, the primary way in which pranayama affects us is on the energetic level.

The word pranayama is usually translated as breath control, but when the word is broken down we can see just how intimately this practice relates to our subtle body. The first part of the word is prana, which means 'life force' and the second part, yama, literally means 'extension.' Therefore, pranayama is the practice of extending or amplifying one's life force.

In order to do this, we need to provide a big enough container to hold the life force. In Chapter Three I discussed the 72,000 nadis and the seven major chakras which carry prana throughout the body. I also talked about the idea that these nadis and chakras can get blocked with mental and emotional baggage causing illness, dysfunction and fatigue. Therefore, pranayama is used first to clear these blockages and then to fill our container.

The practice of pranayama does this very effectively because it is specifically designed to clear the nadis and flood them with life force. This improves our physical stamina, our mental focus and our emotional wellbeing. In so doing it opens the path to spiritual evolution.

Dirga Pranayama

The first step in creating a deep and rich pranayama practice is to learn to deepen the breath. The primary technique for doing this is dirga pranayama. This technique seeks to maximize the capacity of the lungs so we have a system that is filled with life force.

Most people don't breathe deeply at all. In fact, many people use only one fifth of their lung capacity. Most of us are aware that we have two lungs, but our awareness of just how big those lungs are, and the anatomy of the lungs, remains very much a mystery. The lungs extend from the bottom edge of the rib cage to just under the clavicle (collarbone). They also reach quite deeply from front to back. This makes for a lot of room for inhalation and exhalation.

Another fact that surprises many people is that the two lungs are not the same. The right lung has three lobes or compartments whereas the left lung has only two. This is to allow space for the heart on the left side of the body. Although we have separate compartments within our lungs, we tend to use only one lobe per lung at a time. It's a very inefficient use of potential.

We start any pranayama practice by learning to use the lungs fully and completely. The primary technique for doing this is dirga pranayama, which is frequently called 'the complete breath.' In dirga pranayama, we very consciously fill all the lobes of the lungs and very purposefully empty them.

In doing this technique, we accomplish two very important things. First, we bring vast amounts of prana into the body, flooding the nadis with life force. This doesn't remove the blockages in those nadis per se, but it does start things moving again. It's like a good hard rain that fills a dry creek bed. It may not remove all the twigs and brush, but it's an essential first step to moving things through.

The second thing this complete breath does is to exchange apana for prana. Apana is often referred to as the 'downward breath' and is associated with the exhalation. Because its function is to evacuate toxins, it's often associated with something bad. This is a very unfortunate perception. Apana is the counterpoint to the breath of life. Without the sunset, we could not have the sunrise. Without low tide we could not have high tide, and without apana, we could not have prana.

Apana is the essential part of the breath that releases emotional, mental and physical toxins from the system and makes room for new life to enter. This is why it is essential to exhale completely. When we only half exhale, we don't release all that toxic energy, and we don't make space for the next inhalation to fill the body. This creates a subconscious but very real sense of suffocation and lack.

To try dirga pranayama, exhale completely. As you inhale, bring the breath slowly down to the bottom of the lungs so that the belly puffs out a bit. As the lower part of the lungs fill, bring the breath up into the middle section of the lungs and then to the top of the lungs near the collarbone. When you exhale, do it in reverse order by releasing from the top, then the middle, and finally the bottom of the lungs. Although this is a very deep breath, it's not forceful. Try to make the breath slow and mindful. If you can, close your eyes and do this ten times; notice how much different you feel.

Ujjayi Pranayama

Filling the body with oxygen and prana is only the first step, however. Learning to direct the flow of life force consciously is the next step, and this is most often accomplished through ujjayi pranayama. Ujjayi pranayama is often referred to as the ocean sounding breath, though I like to refer to it as the 'Darth Vader breath' because of the hissing sound that's created.

Ujjayi pranayama is practiced by slightly engaging the throat muscles, which enables the yogi to direct that particular breath to any area of the body. This type of breath is frequently used in conjunction with hatha yoga poses. By opening an area of the body, with its related nadis and chakras, in a pose and then directing the ujjayi pranayama to the area being opened, a direct flow of prana is brought to that area. This can be likened to a water pick used on the teeth. The water pick sprays a stream of water onto and between the teeth to remove food and plaque. In ujjayi pranayama we are directing a stream of prana to a given area to help rinse away energetic 'plaque.'

Kapalabhati Pranayama

While the direct flow of prana is very effective in blasting away some energetic impurities, it is not always enough. This is where kapalabhati pranayama is implemented. This technique is frequently referred to as the breath of fire, or the skull polishing breath.

In kapalabhati breathing, the diaphragm muscle at the base of the lungs is willfully pulled toward the spine, forcing all the air from the lungs. As the diaphragm relaxes, the lungs are naturally filled with air. This is generally repeated in fairly rapid succession, creating little puffs of air by an action similar to a bellows. The effect is to push prana throughout the entire energy body. The technique can be likened to the use of a plunger on a clogged drain. Within the plumbing of our energy body, there can be large blockages that will not move easily. Using kapalabhati pranayama is like taking a plunger to those clogs and using the pumping action to free the blockages.

A second benefit of kapalabhati pranayama is that it helps to waken the kundalini energy at the base of the spine. It's like gently nudging the sleeping serpent, encouraging her to wake up and begin her ascent up the spine.

While most of the early stages of yoga focus on teaching us to deepen the breath as much as possible, the more advanced pranayama techniques often include regulating the breath in some way. The practice of regulating the breath is called kumbhaka or breath retention. This breath retention involves regulating the pace of the breath, and at times holding the breath in or out. Given the amount of attention I have just paid to breathing deep and slow, this may seem like a contradiction, but it's the next logical step in the pranayama practice. The breath is much more than a physical act. It's the core of who we are, and it's the place where Spirit and matter come together.

When we really uncover all our judgments, ego projections and energetic blocks, we find that they all spring from one basic delusion: the delusion that we are separate and finite. Our natural response to this belief is fear— both the fear of death and the fear of life. These fears are encompassed in the breath, and as a result, we most often breathe from the ego.

By learning to regulate the breath and hold it peacefully, we free the mind from the constant control of the ego and create space for the Sadguru to take over. Of course, this means we walk headfirst into our deepest fears and most cherished judgments. This is why preparation is recommended before we are taught more advanced techniques, such as analome valome and kumbhaka. Breaking through that primal fear is a big undertaking and one that should only be taken in a safe environment and with an experienced teacher. Nevertheless, these advanced techniques offer the urban mystic very real tools for finding liberation.

More than any other technique offered in yoga, our learning how to use the breath consciously gets us in touch with our spiritual nature. It's the key that unlocks the door to the hidden realm of the soul. Cultivating a rich pranayama practice provides the urban mystic with a major steppingstone on the journey through the eight limbs.

CHAPTER NINE

PRATYAHARA
Sense Withdrawal

◆

"Pleasures conceived in the world of the senses have a beginning and an end and give birth to misery...
The wise do not look for happiness in them."
—BHAGAVAD GITA 5:22

THE WORLD WE SEE

"The yogi in samadhi knows neither heat nor cold,
misery nor happiness, honor nor dishonor."
—HATHA YOGA PRADIPIKA 4:111

Most of us look out at our lives and see a world that seems cruel sometimes and kind at other times. We see a world filled with pain and joy. Sometimes this world seems fair, and at other times very unfair, and depending on what we see in our world, we decide what our experiences are going to be. In fact, most of the time we are searching outside ourselves for a situation that will improve our mood or enhance our attitude.

The problem with all this searching is that the seeds of unhappiness and discontent are not planted in an external garden. They are planted in the field of our individual and collective minds. All suffering begins at the level of the mind; therefore the only logical place where we can alleviate suffering is in the mind. Seeking outside for a solution to suffering is a guarantee that peace and contentment will remain elusive because the problem does not lie within the external circumstances.

Allowing yourself to continue to search outside your mind for the right set of circumstances is like planting an apple seed and hoping to see a banana tree grow. The seeds that are planted in our consciousness are the seeds that will bear fruit in our lives. Yet most people new to the spiritual path look around them and see all sorts of reasons why they cannot be content and at peace.

It seems to be the money, the relationship, the family, or the state of affairs in the world that prevent a person from finding peace. The ego would have us cling to these external things, which it holds up as proof that happiness can only be experienced in brief glimpses. Still the search goes on and on in an endless pursuit.

Yoga seeks to completely invert this way of thinking. This may seem like an extreme statement, but actually it's quite logical. All our suffering originates in the mind, and gets projected outward. Logically then, it's the mind that needs to be changed. The only way to do this is to bring our attention inward. This inward focus is completely opposite to what the ego would have us do.

Pratyahara, the fifth limb of yoga, is where we begin to do this. Pratyahara is the practice of withdrawing the senses and pulling our attention inward. Most of us have been projecting outward for so long, we don't even know we're doing it. Our eyes, ears, nose, mouth and hands seem like peepholes that report what is on the outside, but they are really the ego's tools for projecting everything outward.

This outward projection is the primary way the ego ensures we remain deluded. Only the truly numb can deny we are all searching for something. As long as we deny our true nature, we will feel within us an emptiness that is intolerable. This desire to search is the most natural thing, and it's the unavoidable result of believing that we are not whole. If there must be a search, the ego compromises—it has us search where we will never find what we are looking for.

I often compare the practice of pratyahara to fly-fishing. In fly-fishing, the angler casts the line out and then reels it back in almost as soon as it touches the water. This ongoing process of casting out and reeling back is like the practice of pratyahara, in that the ego is always casting the mind out and Spirit is always reeling it back in.

Once we realize that allowing the mind to be distracted by outside things is the way the ego keeps us in bondage, it's tempting to get caught up in judgment. It's the nature of the ego to cast the mind out, just as the angler casts out his or her line. There is no doubt that this will happen. Rather than judge the process, it's far more useful to allow Spirit to reel the mind back in. Just as the angler understands that the process of casting out and reeling back in is an ongoing process that will continue until the fishing is over, the spiritual seeker needs to understand that the process of the ego's distraction and the return to Spirit is a life-long process.

THE SENSE ORGANS AND ——— SPIRITUAL VISION

"When consciousness internalizes
by uncoupling from external objects, the senses do likewise;
this is called withdrawal of the senses."

—YOGA SUTRA 2:54

The other day I saw a billboard aimed at dispelling some of the myths about HIV and AIDS. Its caption simply read, "How do you know what you know?" The whole idea was that people make certain assumptions about HIV based on unproven facts and hearsay.

It occurred to me that this very simple question would make a great mantra to accompany the practice of pratyahara. So many times we see, hear or feel something, then filter that sensation through our perception and call it truth. The question, "How do you know what you know?" becomes very important when we realize that most of what we think we know is tainted by the ego and is therefore very delusional.

There is a Buddhist story of three blind men who are asked to describe an elephant. The first one feels the tail and says, "An elephant is like a snake." The second one feels the elephant's leg and says, "An elephant is like the trunk of a great tree." The third one feels the ear and says, "An elephant is like a giant palm tree with large leaves."

This is how the ego uses our senses. It allows us to cast the senses out and use them to take in half-truths and partial images. It then reconstructs these images to form a reality that proves its core belief in separateness. This process causes us to walk through life thinking we have a clear picture, but really we have a very deluded perception that keeps us holding fast to our individual and collective illusions.

In order to do this, the ego uses the sense organs. The sense organs are our eyes, ears, nose, mouth and skin. They function as scanning devices that bring information about the outside world into the brain, where we can interpret and act on it. When used properly, these sense organs are very useful, and can be a great tool as we travel through the world. Far too often though, they become tools of the ego and actually work to keep us in bondage.

In the early stages of our yoga practice one of the primary functions of the practice of pratyahara is to gain a deeper awareness of the sense organs. It's not until we do this that we can begin to transcend them. Many of us have turned the sense organs over to the ego to such an extent that we've deadened them. We have built up such a tolerance for pain in our lives that we hardly realize just how much abuse the ego has been inflicting.

This is why the first step in a hatha yoga practice is to get people back into their bodies and into feeling what is happening there. A lot of times the early part of a new yoga practice is simply assessing the damage. Even though this can be a very exciting time in a person's practice, it can also be overwhelming because all the sensations that the ego has been talking circles around come into full awareness.

For example, each time I eat greasy fried foods, my body responds with a stomachache, indigestion and lethargy. My sense organs are telling me something very important: namely that fried food is not good for me. But for a long time I ignored those messages. As I have learned to listen to my body, I find that I am happier and healthier without all that heavy food, and I choose to eat a healthier diet most of the time. Luckily, I learned to listen before that indigestion turned into heart disease, ulcers, cancer, or something similar.

The ego will use the sense organs (our natural body signals) to its own advantage. This is why so many people feel that eating 'healthy food' is a sacrifice and 'unhealthy food' is a treat. Of course, it's not just food—the way we drive, the air we breathe, and the way we feel when we spend too much time in front of the TV—are all examples of the ego at work.

Once we bring awareness back to our senses we can begin to transcend them and tap more and more into our spiritual vision. Transcending the sense organs is not about calling them bad. The sense organs are designed to bring us information about the physical universe, but they are not there to guide us spiritually. Transcending the sense organs is more about knowing what to use and when.

I sometimes compare spiritual vision to the Global Positioning System (GPS). The satellites that orbit our planet are far above the Earth and can therefore pinpoint our exact locations and construct maps to help us navigate. Communication is improved because the satellites are above the fray. Our spiritual vision works in much the same way. Using just the sense organs, we have a limited view of what lies ahead and where we are in relation to the bigger picture.

Many times, the sense organs and spiritual vision will agree. Once, when a friend and I were working on a project together, we had very different ways of making decisions. She is a very analytical person. If we were faced with a decision, she would do some market research or crunch some numbers. I, on the other hand, was more likely to pray and meditate and try to tap into my spiritual vision. She and I didn't always agree on what direction to take, but a surprising amount of the time we did.

When we really listen to our sense organs and take them out of the hands of the ego, they will frequently lead us in the same direction as our spiritual vision. It's important to note that the sense organs and spiritual vision don't always agree. For example, your spiritual vision may be telling you to fast while your sense organs are screaming,

"Hunger!" In these cases I believe it is wise to yield to your spiritual vision.

I have heard this process compared to a court of law. In this court, the Sadguru is the defense attorney and the ego is the prosecutor. The ego takes the facts that the sense organs gather and mixes them up to confuse the jury, and the Sadguru calmly brings things back into focus when we give Her a chance to speak. That focus and clarity are what spiritual vision offers, and the practice of pratyahara gives this Great Teacher a chance to show you the evidence in a new way.

CRAVING AND AVERSION

"Two birds of beautiful plumage, comrades inseparable, live on the selfsame tree. One bird eats the fruit of pleasure and pain; the other looks on without eating."

—SHVETASHVATARA UPANISHAD 4:6

Craving and aversion are the two basic ways in which the ego seeks to keep us in a mode of outward projection and thus prevent us from looking within. Although we seem to have a wide range of sensory desires, there are only these two. By splitting our sensory desires into many different subcategories, the ego causes our sense projections to seem warranted and natural. But no matter how diverse the ego thinks your desires to be, they always come back to craving and aversion.

It is essential to understand our habitual tendency to crave certain things and avoid others if we truly want to reel the sense organs back in and regain control over the mind. The cleverly cloaked insanity of the ego becomes bitterly apparent when we take a close look at our desires, and we then take a major step towards undoing the ego's most basic line of defense—projection. In order to do this, however, we need to look closely at craving and aversion, the foundation of the ego's projections.

In reality, craving and aversion are flip sides of the same coin, and this becomes more and more apparent as one becomes more skilled at practicing pratyahara. What is one man's pleasure is another man's pain, so to speak. Craving and aversion are defined only by a series of ego judgments, yet they seem to be quite different. Both have equal ability to keep us in delusion, and though they are really one and the same, it's helpful in the beginning to look at them separately.

Soon after I moved to San Francisco, a friend took me to the Folsom Street Fair. Every year, each of San Francisco's diverse neighborhoods takes a Sunday afternoon to showcase the unique style and flavor of the neighborhood. The Folsom Street fair is known for its celebration of the leather and S&M communities; consequently, it can be quite shocking for those whose sexual interests are more traditional.

I am far from a sexual prude myself, but I have never really understood the dynamics of pain in the context of sexuality. Although I had always tried not to judge the sexuality of others, S&M had always seemed like something that a person would do to fill some deep psychological void.

On this day, however, I was forced to look at my judgments. Everyone was dressed in leather and sporting whips, handcuffs and an assortment of other items with which to bind, beat and humiliate. My ego was going crazy. It seemed almost impossible not to go into judgment about what was happening all around me.

Then we stopped at a booth where a woman was tied to a post and a large man with a leather mask was flogging her. I flinched as the tassels snapped against her back, turning her skin a bright shade of pink. I was raised to believe that it was wrong to hit another person, and this was doubly true if that person was a girl. Watching this was extremely challenging. I wanted to call 911 or find some way to help this poor woman.

My lesson that day came when he untied her and she turned around. I had expected to see makeup running down her face from tears of pain. But what I saw was a woman who was extremely satisfied. For her, this experience seemed to be every bit as pleasurable as traditional sex is for me.

It was in watching her that I started to realize that pleasure and pain are really all in the mind and are strongly influenced by the ego's cravings and aversions. I'm still not turned on by the S&M experience, but it's no longer necessary for me to judge it. I now understand there is a fine line between pleasure and pain, and it's most often defined by the craving and aversion principle to which the ego adheres so closely.

While my ego tells me that tender touching and gentle kissing bring about pleasure, her ego was telling her that getting flogged was giving her a good time. My point in telling this story is to recognize that pleasure and pain are defined by the ego, and thus the way to transcend the ego is to step back. We need to stop chasing after sensations that the ego calls good, and to stop running away from the sensations that the ego calls bad.

When we allow the ego's craving to rule the mind, we seek out pleasure as the ego defines it. As we have just noted, pleasure is something that is defined, for the most part, on an individual basis. Of course our family and cultural experience will have a lot to do with how we define pleasure, but ultimately our individual egos define what we crave and then send us out in a never-ending search.

Pleasure in and of itself is not a bad thing. Enjoying sensations on the level of the body is a wonderful part of being human. It's not until the ego latches on to a natural craving and uses it to distract us that it becomes a problem. Food, for instance, can be a very pleasurable part of being in the body, and having an appetite is a good thing, because it tells us when to eat. But when the ego warps that natural desire for food, it turns appetite into a craving that can never really be satisfied.

This is why that hot fudge sundae feels so good going down, but quickly turns into a leash. When we chase after that pleasure without first finding contentment within, we deny ourselves the opportunity to really enjoy the food, but when we find contentment within, we can enjoy the sensual pleasures of life without being chained to them.

Sexuality is another great example. The many forms of sex can be a source of great pleasure. It doesn't matter if you're gay or straight, kinky or reserved. What matters is why you're seeking sex. Many times people want sex to fill an emotional void or create a distraction from some sort of pain. When we seek sex for such reasons as these, we tend to feel drained and depleted. This is also why sex can create such conflict within relationships.

Growing up, I spent a lot of time on my father's farm. Every spring the animals would mate. There was no shame or guilt, and the animals didn't spend all their free time chasing after sex. When the time is right, the animals mate, and when the time is not right, they go back to grazing. This is because animals don't have over-inflated egos. They don't have an agenda; they simply do what is natural.

If you take a moment to review your life, you will likely find many areas where your ego has sent you on wild tangents seeking out physical pleasure. If you're content within, then the sex, food and other physical experiences you seek can be a great affirmation of your innate wholeness. But when the ego turns that natural desire into a craving, it becomes perverted and serves to distract us from the knowledge of Atman.

Aversion is not much different. As we walk through life, there are multitudes of things that keep us running. On a physical level, we avoid many healthy foods, telling ourselves they are not tasty, or we may avoid ending a painful relationship because of the emotional challenges. People will often stay in jobs that are unsatisfying because they're afraid, or they feel the need for security.

All these things are ways the ego uses the aversion principle in order to run the show. By keeping us running away from the uncomfortable, we often miss the lesson. When something makes us uncomfortable, it's generally because we need to look at it. This is why yoga encourages us to look at the uncomfortable sensation, rather than avoid it. Pain is the doorway out of pain.

Imagine you had chronic headaches. You could spend your life taking aspirin and other painkillers. This would no doubt help to alleviate the pain, but it would deny you the opportunity to explore the situation in depth. Perhaps your headaches are stress related, or perhaps they are due to a more serious problem. Whatever the case, avoiding them will not solve the problem. Looking at the message they bring may well offer a solution.

Every time we find ourselves avoiding something, we are running away from who we are. We are subtly saying, "I will not be happy until this situation changes." But even when the situation changes, we will begin looking again. Like the headache, pain on any level tells us that something is out of balance. By learning to sit with the uncomfortable, we have the opportunity to gain deep insights into the nature of our suffering.

My friend Michael called me the other day. He told me he was quitting his job because he was so unhappy. I was somewhat surprised because he had a good job that paid well. I asked him how he planned to pay the rent, and he said, "I have no idea, but that lump in my throat disappeared when I made my decision. I don't know what's next, but I know I made the right choice."

You could hear the peace in his voice. He had spent years avoiding the fear of letting go of his job. That aversion was what had kept him so unhappy, but when he really sat with that fear, it disappeared. He no longer had to make excuses for the job he hated and was ready to move on to whatever his spirit had in store for him.

This is how the ego uses craving and aversion. When the ego is running the show we are caught in an endless cycle of running away from that which the ego calls uncomfortable and chasing after that which the ego calls pleasurable. This ensures that we never stop long enough to remember who we are, and simultaneously gives us the illusion that we are doing something to quell that nagging sense of dissatisfaction that haunts so many of our hours.

Learning to practice pratyahara, then, is the key to delving deeper into the mind and finding that inner peace about which we have been talking. Until we learn to reel the mind back in, that sense of peace will always be just out of reach, but once we do, the return to our ecstatic center is only a matter of time.

— THE THREE STEPS OF PRATYAHARA —

"Attachment is that which dwells upon pleasure.
Aversion is that which dwells upon pain."
—YOGA SUTRA 2:7-8

Step One

When we start a hatha yoga practice, one of the first things we do is begin to develop body awareness. This may seem like a strange thing to develop, since we live in our bodies all day long. But even though we have all lived in our bodies from birth, a surprising number of people are completely out of touch with the muscles and bones they call home.

Getting back in touch with the body is the first step in the practice of pratyahara. Until we arrive in the physical and bring it to conscious awareness, there is little that can be done to move beyond the physical and into the realm of the mind. For most of us, this process of deepening body awareness happens in three phases. First, we become aware of aches and pains in the body. Most of us come to a yoga practice because we've let our bodies fall victim to neglect. Stress, poor eating habits and a sedentary way of life all do untold damage to the body.

After years of letting the ego run the body, many of us show up on the yoga mat feeling like dilapidated old buildings that are no longer safe to enter. So when we do enter the body with full awareness, what we find can be quite alarming. Our awareness is frequently accompanied by depression, because the amount of damage done to the body can be overwhelming. Luckily, the body is quite resilient, and healing can progress quite quickly.

Once we arrive in the body and sit in a state of overwhelm for a bit, we begin the next phase—prioritizing needs. Perhaps we will start with small steps like taking vitamin supplements or eating a bit better. Eventually we listen to the body more and more until the bigger things like smoking and drinking are dismissed. For most people this process comes about quickly, because it's impossible to be consciously in the body without feeling divided while living in denial of its needs.

When I first started taking yoga, I was a two-pack-a-day smoker. I didn't quit after my first class, but it was not long before I really started to feel the negative effects of smoking on a conscious level. The increase in body awareness made it more and more difficult to ignore what smoking was doing to my body. In time I did quit, and I credit my decision to quit largely to the increased body awareness I had started to develop in yoga.

Once we clean up our lifestyles and undo some of the basic damage that years of neglect and abuse have left behind, we enter into a stage of conscious dialog with the body. The body knows what it needs, and during this level of body awareness, we enter into the practice of listening to the messages of the body on a moment-to-moment basis. In so doing, we are always making subtle adjustments to our behavior so that the body can be fully supported.

Step Two

The second step in the practice of pratyahara is going into the sensation. In the first step we became aware of the sensations of the body, and we raised our body awareness. In this next step we willfully and consciously bring the mind into the sensation. In doing this we begin to look at the nature and origin of the sensation and what is behind it.

We have this natural tendency to crave certain sensations and avoid others. Thus, we exploit that which the ego deems as good, and avoid at all costs that which the ego deems bad. This prevents us from going beyond the ego's judgments.

When we are on the yoga mat, we intentionally put ourselves in poses that are uncomfortable. These poses, when practiced with the proper instruction and a degree of mindfulness, are very safe. Yet, even though they're safe, the ego will go crazy with judgments.

Of course, some poses will come easily and others will be more difficult, but, when it comes to pratyahara, your level of skill in any given pose is not the issue. The key to practicing pratyahara at this level is in finding an edge. The edge is that place in a pose where things are intense, but not so intense that one is risking injury. It's this edge that triggers the ego's craving and aversion response.

As the ego starts its usual routine of looking for ways to make the pose more comfortable (or avoid it all together), we can begin to practice pratyahara more fully. It is here you have a choice. You can obey the ego and allow it to continue to be the master, or you can sit in the pose and enter the doorway of sensation.

Behind all the drama that the ego kicks up around yoga poses there is liberation from that drama. The ego's like the wizard in The Wizard of Oz in that it loves to have us pay attention to the smoke and flames, rather than look behind the curtain. When we go into the sensation, we get to pull back the curtain and see exactly what is behind it.

When I first began yoga, there was one pose, the locust (shalabhasana) that I disliked above all others. I was convinced that Ellie, my teacher, knew this and would do it every time I was in class, just to be mean. What was interesting was that whenever Ellie would instruct us to take that pose, my bladder would magically fill, and I would have to go to the bathroom. It never occurred to me that it was my ego, looking for a way to avoid that pose. Because I was unaware of the reason for my full bladder, I would conveniently excuse myself each time she called for that pose. Eventually I started to catch on, and began to stay for the pose. It wasn't easy at first and I still struggle with it, but by staying with the sensation, I have found that it has become much easier and I have been able to work through layers of fear that I didn't even know were there.

One thing I often say to my students is, "Look for the smile behind the sensation." To find liberation from the cravings and aversions of the ego, we must go through them. The way we do this is by finding the uncomfortable, sitting with it, and breathing into it.

This works just as well in life as it does on the yoga mat. My friend Sue has struggled with compulsive overeating for many years. At her heaviest, she was 345 pounds. She came to me for private yoga sessions for awhile and eventually accepted my offer to show her a yoga-based diet that would help improve her health and lose some weight. As I outlined what she would need to do, she started to shut down and get depressed.

"I can't do this. The cravings will be too great," she said. I asked her to calm down and take a few breaths. I then explained that she needed not only to change her diet, but also change her mind. I told her, "The problem you have is not with the food. The problem is in the cravings that you keep giving in to. There is something behind that craving that your ego doesn't want you to see. And the only way you're going to be able to look at it is by going through the cravings without giving in to them."

Sue agreed to try. I told her that she needed to combine her new diet with a daily practice of gentle yoga and meditation, and that she needed to pray and meditate before each meal. She still struggles with her diet and the cravings associated with food, but to date she has lost more than 100 pounds and she continues to lose. More important than the weight loss, she is happy again and making great strides in her personal growth and spiritual practice.

Step Three

The third step in practicing pratyahara is complete sense withdrawal. It's in this phase of the practice that pratyahara's true rewards are experienced. At this level the yogi pulls the senses in to such a degree that he or she is completely unaffected by external things.

I've heard this phase of the practice being compared to a turtle that has withdrawn into its shell, and this is a very apt metaphor. That's exactly what the experience feels like. When we shut down the sense organs, we move the awareness out of external projections into the inner realm where all those projections originate.

When I first heard about this pratyahara practice, I was going to a lot of twelve-step meetings and the word denial was tossed around quite a bit. It seemed to me that this practice of shutting out the outside world was no more than a glorified form of denial. It seemed more like an ostrich sticking its head in the sand than a spiritual practice. But this is not the case at all; it is quite the opposite.

As we have noted over and over, the illusion of maya, which makes up our external world, is based on the projections of our collective and individual egos. The ego creates this illusion in order to prevent us from looking at and transcending its erroneous thought system. This is why the ego is so insistent on having us stay in an outwardly focused mode.

There is a Buddhist story about a man running into a burning house and rearranging the furniture rather than help people escape. This is what the ego would have us do. Rather than look at the real cause of our suffering, the ego has us rearrange the details of maya. When we do this we are living in denial of the true cause of suffering.

From this point of view then, withdrawing the senses and moving into the final stage of pratyahara is the opposite of denial. We are in denial when we look outside for answers and solutions. When we stop looking without and go completely within, we get to look at the real issues that cause suffering.

The first time I experienced this level of sense withdrawal, I was in the middle of a weeklong fast. The first few days of any fast are always difficult, but I had made it through and was finding it easier and easier.

During this fast I had cut back my workload and lengthened my daily yoga and meditation practice. On day number five, while sitting to meditate during my afternoon practice, I was confronted with waves of hunger. These hunger pains were unexpected because I thought I was through the worst of it. They were so strong, however, that I almost left the meditation to go to the kitchen.

Somehow, perhaps by grace, I managed to stay. Rather than avoid the hunger, I decided to meditate on it—bringing my attention to it while at the same time not allowing my mind to sink into drama about it. It was hard, but it allowed me to do something with the hunger rather than simply dwell in it. Over time the hunger changed forms and became less intense. I was able to smile at it, and its bite was not so sharp.

Then something happened. The hunger stopped altogether. But it wasn't just the hunger; it was also the sounds of the room; they had always been in my peripheral awareness, but now the sensation of the air touching my skin, the light hitting my eyelids, the smells of the room, all were gone. They weren't just in the distant background; they were gone. You'd think that I would have been frightened by this event, but it never occurred to me that it was anything but natural. I was very much at peace with the experience, and I was in no hurry for it to end. In fact, time had very little meaning that afternoon.

For the first time in my life I started to see how much my definition of myself was based on sensory experience, and in this new space none of that external self-definition was available to my ego. I had to be me, in and of myself; it was quite liberating.

A few years earlier I had had a dream that I was in my childhood home. As I walked through the living room, I noticed a door I had never seen before. It struck me as odd, even within the dream, that I could live my life in this house and overlook the most obvious door. I walked through the door to find many rooms and corridors that were new to me. There was so much to explore and find, but I woke up before I could really map out this newfound wing in my home.

My experience with pratyahara that day was a lot like this dream. I had spent my whole life led by my senses, never really noticing they were a doorway into a vast inner world. I never even knew the door was there, but once I found it and walked through, I began to see just how big and vast my mind really was. Just as my childhood home seemed so small after that dream, my little external world shrank that day I experienced pratyahara.

Many of the great yogis can enter at will into a state of complete sense withdrawal, and can shut out the external world without much effort. I'm not always able to enter into this deep level of pratyahara. I wouldn't even say that I go there often. But once I found that door and walked through it, something changed for me, in that my focus in life became decidedly more inward.

This door is not an exit; it's an entrance. When we walk through it, we are ready to move fully and consciously into the upper three limbs of yoga. This is where the deep work begins. Up to this point we have been working to find the mind and delve into it more consciously. Now that we've entered the realm of the mind, the clutter that has been molding our physical health, emotional stability and mental sanity can be addressed directly, and we can do this each time we walk through pratyahara's door.

CHAPTER TEN

DHARANA
Concentration

"Concentration locks consciousness on a single area."
—YOGA SUTRA 3:1

CONCENTRATION

"He who binds the breath, binds the mind. He who binds the mind, binds the breath. The breath dissolves where the mind dissolves. The mind dissolves where the breath dissolves."
—HATHA YOGA PRADIPIKA 4:21-22

Once we have learned, through the practice of pratyahara, to pull the mind back in, we begin the next limb of our practice. The sixth limb, dharana, is about learning to focus the mind. For many of us, this is the most difficult part of the whole practice, because here in our Western culture, concentration is not something that is taught from a young age. When it comes to dharana we are like that proverbial old dog trying to learn new tricks. Ours is a culture that over stimulates the brain with the flashy and the neon. We plop our kids down in front of programs like Sesame Street, which use bright numbers and colorful symbols to maintain the attention of the young minds that watch it. Of course, some children's programs do help their education tremendously, but the constant flashiness of our society makes it hard to stay focused on the small and mundane.

Consequently, most of us have not learned how to focus the mind or live in the present moment. Our urban lives often involve a sense of rush and hurry that make it all too easy to overlook the simple and small things. So many of us view life at such a rapid pace that it streaks past in a blur.

Learning to concentrate is key, because if we don't, the ego will distract us again and again. The ego loves to distract the seeker from her purpose. As long as we hop from one thought to the next without ever knowing how that thought entered the mind, we will not be able to cut through the underlying misperceptions of the ego and experience Atman.

The mind is often compared to a beam of light, and this image works very well when we explore the practice of dharana. There are really only two ways we can use light. The first is in a beam, such as the light of a flashlight. This beam of light starts at a single point and grows wider as it leaves the source. The other way, a laser, is just the opposite. Unlike a flashlight, which starts at a small point and then diffuses as it travels outward, the laser is focused light. It keeps moving inward toward a specific point, and thus maintains its strength and focus. This is what gives it the ability to do everything from reading a compact disk to correcting the vision in many people's eyes.

When we practice dharana, we are shifting the way we use the mind. Like pratyahara, we are completely inverting the way the mind works under the ego's reign. The ego would have us use the mind in flashlight mode, while Spirit would have us focus the mind and use its incredible power as a very precise tool to cut through illusion.

In previous chapters we have used the image of the river, but as we look at the practice of dharana, this image becomes even more meaningful. The practice of concentration brings the banks of our river closer together. Prior to engaging in this practice, the mind somewhat resembles a great swamp filled with stagnant water. As we begin to move the banks of the river inward, the waters of consciousness move more swiftly, providing a powerful force that can be used to mold and shape our external world while at the same time speeding up our journey toward Self-realization.

Dharana brings order to the jumble of thoughts and judgments that clutter the conscious and unconscious mind. It's like looking at a very messy and disorganized room. Initially, there is the temptation to sit in a state of overwhelm and ignore the chore of organizing. But when you focus and you put things in place one at a time, the job gets done quickly and effectively. Cleaning out the mind is no different. The task can be quite daunting, but when we concentrate and focus, the work moves swiftly. Without that deep level of concentration, however, it's unlikely that much will change.

- THERE'S NO TIME BUT THE PRESENT -

"There is the form and expression that we call 'past', and the form and expression we call 'future'; both exist within the object, at all times. Form and expression vary according to time—past, present and future."
—YOGA SUTRA 4:12

Just as pratyahara offered us a doorway out of the physical by moving more consciously into sensation, the practice of dharana offers us a similar door. This door does not lead us out of the physical, but rather out of time.

As you may recall, one of the essential aspects of Atman is its timeless nature. Like God, each of us is an eternal being, yet we've been deluded into believing that we are finite. Each of us has bought a piece of real estate in the world of time, and it has been a very bad investment.

We live our lives as if there were a beginning and an end to who we are, and we live as if death were the only thing certain in this world. Indeed, from a bodily point of view, we live very much in the world of time. This is understandable, since we can see time marching on. People are born, age and die—empires rise and fall, everything in this world is limited by time.

We go to great pains to measure time. We have calendars and clocks to mark the days and minutes, and we give great significance to dates that mark the passage of time, such as birthdays, anniversaries, New Year celebrations and new millennia. Time is so much a part of our lives that the thought of stepping outside it seems impossible. In many ways time is the bedrock on which the rest of maya is built.

This is why it's exceedingly difficult to transcend time. Time is so much a part of our psyche that we may wonder why we would even want to transcend it. But time, when used by the ego, is a weapon that keeps us in fear. When the ego uses time, our experience of it is based solely on the judgments of the ego. We never seem to have enough time, but when it moves slowly we can't wait for it to pass.

As a matter of fact, time was a key part of Albert Einstein's theory of relativity. He was once asked to explain this complex theory in terms that the common person could understand. He said, "One minute with your hand on a hot stove would seem like an hour, whereas one hour kissing the woman you love will seem like one minute. That's relativity."

Because our true nature is eternal, the ego needs to keep the mind separate from eternity in order to keep us searching for peace without possibility of success. In order for a person to be separate, he or she must have a beginning and an end. Likewise, in order for us to be limited, time is a prerequisite. In this sense, time is the glue that holds the illusion together.

Just as in every other aspect of yoga, we cannot transcend time by denial. People try to escape the effects of time by using cosmetics and buying fast cars. Of course, none of this works. In effect, when we try to deny the seeming reality of time, we simply make it appear more real.

To a yogi, time is not bad. Actually, time is very useful while we are here in this illusion. Time creates a space for evolution to take place, and offers each of us the opportunity to keep on trying things until we finally choose the peace of our true nature over the insanity of the ego. Again, time is not bad; it's simply not real.

Rather than make time good or bad, yoga helps us to let go of the need for time. This can only be done in the present moment. Just as sensation was the door that led from the external world to our inner world, the practice of dharana leads us through the door of the present moment into the realm of eternity.

The ego seeks to have us live in the past or in the future because we will never find eternity there. That's why every mystical tradition places such strong emphasis on staying present. The present moment is the only time when we can enter into eternal bliss. Enlightenment is not something that comes after many lifetimes; it's a decision we make now.

Bringing our attention to the present moment is exceptionally difficult when we live in such a fast-paced society. Learning to sit still for even a moment can seem almost impossible. That's why so many people have a hard time maintaining a seated meditation practice. For many of us, our lives seem to move at warp ten and sitting still can feel too overwhelming.

One of the greatest benefits of a hatha yoga practice is that it doesn't require us to sit still. Many of us find sitting still is not a realistic option in the beginning. The mind twists and turns so much that it's very difficult to stay present. Yoga poses and breathing are a bit more active, and this makes it easier.

Life in our modern world often moves like a runaway train. For most of us, it would be too much to jump from this fast-moving train onto a meditation cushion. I see yoga as a truck that pulls up alongside the train and moves at the same speed until we can safely jump off. Then yoga slows down with us on board. In this way, we can gradually move back to the present moment. Once we have slowed down a bit, many of us are also able to start a seated meditation practice.

A second reason why hatha yoga brings the mind to the present moment so effectively is because the body can only be in the moment. The mind can wander into the past or future and will likely spend a good deal of time in one or the other. The body, however, is always in the present. When we bring attention to the body, we have no choice but to bring the mind back to the moment as well. The body can actually act like an anchor, holding the mind in a very present space.

Of course we don't need to wait until we are on our yoga mats or meditation cushions to bring the mind to the present moment. Everything in life can be a meditation. But because most of us are choosing to live in the modern world rather than run off to a cave in the Himalayas, our lives can easily get filled with things that take the mind away from the present moment. Rather than get distracted by these things, we can work to use them as a meditation.

For example, I was at the post office the other day, and as usual, the line was about fifteen people long. To make the situation even more frustrating, there was only one clerk working while two others stood in plain view chatting about something other than work. I could feel the frustration in the air. The woman in front of me shifted anxiously back and forth, and the man in back of me muttered obscenities to himself. I found myself getting sucked into this drama. I could feel tension in my face and neck, and my back molars were pressing firmly against each other. Interestingly, I wasn't in a rush. It was my day off and all I had on my schedule for the day was sitting at a café with my laptop. There was no reason for me to be in a rush, but I was acting as if I had a deep flesh wound and was trying to get to the emergency room.

It took me a few minutes, but I was able to return to my breath. It wasn't easy; my ego wanted so badly to be angry and upset. But I turned that time of waiting into a meditation. By breathing deeply and bringing my mind to the present moment, I was able to calm down and find my center.

Each of the people in front of me took turns attempting to make the clerk feel bad. One man slammed his mail down. The next person refused to talk. By the time I got to the window, I was very centered and present. Not only that, I was able to see the clerk as a hard worker who had the unpleasant job of working alone and dealing with lots of frustrated people. Rather than subtly or overtly insulting her, I decided to thank her for working so hard. The look of complete surprise on her face quickly gave way to a big smile.

The practice of dharana begins in the present moment. The present starts now. We don't need to wait until we are on the yoga mat to arrive in the now. A line at the post office, a red light or a delayed flight are all invitations to practice dharana. When we do this we start to see things as they are in Truth, and every breath becomes a spiritual practice. There is no time where Spirit is not, yet the only way we can realize this is by being in the now.

In his book, The Tao of Healing, Haven Trevino summed this idea up beautifully when he wrote, "Consider it, in this present moment, God chooses to be you."

───────────── **CHOOSING REALITY** ─────────────

"Reshape yourself through the power of the will; never let yourself be degraded by self-will. The will is the only friend of the Self, and the will is the only enemy of the Self."
—BHAGAVAD GITA, 6:5

In the movie, Star Wars: The Phantom Menace, Quigon, a Jedi knight, reminds his young student, Anakin, "Your focus determines your reality." This was very wise advice, even if it did come from a galaxy far, far away. His advice might well have come from a yogi, because it's a fundamental aspect of yogic philosophy that one's mental focus affects reality.

Because the practice of dharana helps us to live more and more in the present moment, we are able to determine the reality in which we find ourselves. Living in the present moment helps us stop and smell the proverbial roses, and in this alone it's a great practice. But the deeper benefits of concentrating your mind in the present moment involve a conscious choice of your reality.

Each of us has created our own reality, and collectively we've chosen a reality that we all share. Until a person starts on the spiritual path, life seems to happen by accident or by fate, but as we become more and more present to life, we see that life is a series of choices that are made in the present moment. For just that reason it's important to bring focus to the present moment. Changing your mind, and consequently changing your reality, can only happen in the present moment. We can spend a lot of time regretting or feeling nostalgic about the past. We can fantasize about the future or live in fear of it. But both the past and future are illusions. The past is gone and the future is nonexistent. Therefore, the only time that exists is now. Because the eternal now is the only time there is, it's the only place where we can change our minds, and the practice of dharana brings us to this present state of mind.

Two years ago I was at a family reunion. These types of things can be fun and intense both at the same time. Visiting with people you haven't seen in years can be great, but there's always so much ground to cover, it's hard to get to any real depth with people.

One of the people I saw at this reunion was one of my mother's cousins whom I had not seen since junior high school. She had had several children and been married and divorced several times. It was great to see her after so many years. We found a patch of shade under a big tree and began to fill each other in on the assorted details of our lives.

As she told me about each of her husbands, I noticed a pattern. Each of her husbands had left her for another woman. This series of negative experiences had left her with the opinion that "men are all jerks." Rather than be insulted by being lumped into the 'jerk' category because of my gender, I decided to explore this belief with her.

She gave me a detailed description of each man. The first husband was a bit on the wild side. He rode a Harley and loved to spend time in bars and pool halls. The second husband was a preppy real-estate agent, and her third husband was a self-help junkie who spent more time in twelve-step meetings than at work. In a way it was amazing that she could find herself attracted to three such completely different types of men. As she continued to tell me about all her bad relationship luck, I could see her dipping deeper and deeper into an ego drama that had a bad tailspin. Since self-pity is like nails on a chalkboard for me, I decided to confront her.

"Do you know what all three of these guys had in common?" I asked. "Other than the fact that they're all pigs, I can't think of much. They were all very different," she replied.

"Actually, they have one very important thing in common. They were all married to you when you decided they were pigs."

"What are you trying to say—that men should be allowed to cheat on women?" she exclaimed.

"Of course not," I replied. "But you are the one who made the choice to date them and then to marry them. You are the one who chooses to hold resentment toward them, and as result, you're going to continue to date men who will validate your belief that 'men are jerks.' If you believe that all men are jerks and pigs, you're going see that everywhere. But if you start to change your mind, I think you'll find that the men you meet in the future will be quite well adjusted and respectful. The key is to change your mind now, rather than wait for some future prince charming to do it for you."

Like my mother's cousin, we're all directing our focus out into the world and seeing the results. If we focus on cheating husbands or negative experiences, that's what we'll unconsciously create in our lives. But if we learn to focus our attention on things that support us and cultivate a spiritual base on which to stand, we'll find more positive experiences.

There's more than just wishful thinking here. How we focus the mind determines how our reality will unfold. This is such an important facet of our spiritual path. Until we learn to focus the mind on the present moment and make conscious choices, we will always feel like the victim of happenstance. We'll always be waiting for the better hand to be dealt us, and even if we get a good hand, we'll live in fear of the next round, because luck has a funny way of running out at the worst possible time. That's why it's so important to see that life is not about luck or fate, but rather about choice.

Right before I started on my spiritual path, I found a woman who read tarot cards. Her reading of me seemed so accurate it was scary. She seemed to know exactly what was going on in my life. Before she laid out each card, she would tell me what it represented. Some had to do with relationships, others with the past or with my self-image. The last card she put down had to do with my future. The card that came up is called The Tower, and it depicts a large stone tower which is crumbling and falling. Flames pour out of the sides and people are falling to their deaths. At the time I didn't know much about tarot, but I knew this didn't look good. She then went on to confirm my suspicion. She told me that the card symbolizes the destruction and breaking down of the old. According to her, this card frequently indicates that a person is holding on to an old way of life that's about to get knocked to the ground.

She could tell I was nervous and uncomfortable with the card, so she took my hand and smiled. She was a large woman, adorned with crystals and new age jewelry. She was odd by my standards, but she had big beautiful blue eyes and locks of blond hair that fell down over her shoulders. As she looked softly at me, she said, "Why are you here?"

"Because I want you to tell me the future, I guess," I responded, though in all honesty I was not really clear about why I was there.

"Well, I can't tell you the future, but I can give you insight as to where you are right now and where you'll go if you stay on your present course. The beauty of a reading like this is that it gives you a snapshot of your life, so you can make changes if you want to. What would be the point in getting a reading if the future were already set in stone? The only thing you can change is the present, but if you're aware, then you can make more informed choices about your life. If you don't want your life to burn and crumble, you need to surrender and let go of things now. The future is created out of the present moment. You need to leave the tower you have built, or you may wind up like one of the people falling from it, and I don't think you want that."

Through the practice of dharana, we bring our minds to the present moment and the current situation. This gives a yogi the most valuable thing in the world—choice.

—— THE THREE LEVELS OF DHARANA ——

"[Concentration] must be applied stage by stage"
—YOGA SUTRA 3:6

When we are on the yoga mat or the meditation cushion, there are several levels to the practice of dharana. Like the practice of pratyahara, each stage needs to be mastered in the moment before we can move on to the next stage. Intention is paramount in this practice. It's not easy to have a focused mind, and it will be impossible if there is no strong intention to return to that focus point. First, we need to choose a focus point—usually the breath or one of the sensations of the body—but it may also be a mantra, prayer, or visualization. The exact focus point is not all that important. What is important is that it be specific. By choosing a set point on which to concentrate, we take the beam of our mental flashlight and focus it inward, turning it into a mental laser.

In the next limb (dhyana/meditation), the focus point will act like a submarine, in that it will be a mechanism that takes our conscious awareness deeper into the mind, allowing the urban mystic to consciously explore the semi-conscious and the unconscious regions which will be explored in the next chapter. For this reason it's important to develop a strong dharana practice—and find a suitable focus point.

As we begin this first step of the dharana practice, it's very tempting to want to check out and go into what I call grocery list mode. This is where we go into the usual ego routine of juggling several things at once. It may seem efficient to be trying to get other things done while you're in your yoga practice, but it simply keeps the mind unfocussed.

When we focus the mind on the sensations of the body and the rhythm of the breath, we give the mind something to hold onto. Because the body is present at all times, we're adding the benefit of keeping the mind in the now. This in turn allows us to make new decisions about how we want to be in our body, while at the same time retraining the mind to be in the present moment.

The second step in dharana is to allow the mind to be single-pointed. If your focus point is the breath, for example, allow the mind to rest on the breath. In the moments where the mind is single-pointed, the ego becomes still and the conscious mind sinks deeper into the unconscious. By keeping the mind single-pointed, the yogi moves fully into the present moment and stands on the threshold of eternity. In this centered space we make room for the final two limbs of yoga (dhyana/meditation and samadhi/ecstasy).

When we realize our mind has wandered away from the focus point, we can enter into the third step—the return. The nature of the ego is to keep us busy. It will look for many ways to distract the yogi, and it will find some really effective ones. Among its chief techniques for keeping us distracted are the craving and aversion principles that we discussed in the last chapter. In this stage the key is to continue to return to the practice without judgment. The ego has had many years to hone its skills. You can be sure it will be very adept at getting the mind to wander off the focus point. You can count on the mind getting distracted almost as much as you can count on the sun coming up every morning.

Never getting distracted is not what the practice of dharana is about. It's about returning to your focus point each time you realize that you have been distracted. When you realize you've let your mind wander, it's very easy to fall into self-judgment for not being totally focused. This serves no purpose at all. It will only keep you from your single-pointed mission of freeing the mind. Remember, no matter how much the mind goes off into thoughts of planning and judging, the practice at this step is to bring it back to the focus point over and over again.

For example, the other day I had some time between classes so I stopped off at Dolores Park. It's one of the great oases in the heart of San Francisco. It has one of the best views of the city, and there are always interesting people there, sunning themselves, walking dogs or playing with their children in the playground.

When I have some time between classes, I often stop at the park, do a mini yoga practice and then sit in meditation. On this day, I was having a good practice as far as the physical poses were concerned. My body seemed to be cooperating, but my mind would not stay present. Over and over again I would find myself planning my next class, or reworking and mentally editing the article I had been writing about natural alternatives to Viagra. One thing in my favor was my awareness that my mind was wandering, and because I realized this, I was able to practice the three steps of dharana more consciously.

I use the breath as a focus point, so I focused my mind on the breath flowing in and out. Though my intentions were good, I was easily distracted by the very attractive assortment of scantily clad sunbathers who were all around me. However, I kept returning to the breath. Then a very cute dog came up and waited for me to play with her. She rolled around and used the 'dog' eyes that I find so hard to resist. I continued to return to my breath, though it felt like a hopeless cause. It took the better part of the practice, but eventually I slipped into a very focused space while in the dancer pose. My mind slipped into a state where it was so focused on the moment that time seemed to stretch on forever. I felt my leg and foot lift higher and higher over my head and I could feel my standing leg reaching deeply into the earth. Because I was so focused, I was able to make subtle adjustments to the pose that brought it to a new depth. Although I held the pose for less than a minute, the time seemed to be irrelevant. My mind, for that brief moment, was in the now, and I was able to sink deeper into my unconscious mind.

The practice of dharana has a very definite application in a hatha yoga practice, but it doesn't need to end there. In fact, it can be applied effectively to any aspect of life. When we keep returning to a focus point in life, everything we do becomes a spiritual practice. Imagine if doing the laundry, cooking a meal or driving a car were as therapeutic as doing the dancer pose. Indeed, they can become spiritually centering if they're done with the mindfulness of dharana.

There's a story about a Christian monk who became enlightened when doing the dishes. Although all his fellow brothers were delighted to have him do their dishes for them, they naturally thought he was a bit odd. To him, however, washing dishes was a great opportunity to practice mindfulness. He became Self-realized by being present to the dishes.

As urban mystics this becomes a great asset for us. Most of us will not be spending six hours a day in a formal spiritual practice. Realistically, we'll be spending about ninety minutes in a guided yoga practice each day. Some people may practice even less. That doesn't mean we can't turn many of our day-to-day activities into a yoga practice.

Brushing your teeth, eating in silence, or being present to a child can all provide great opportunities to center the mind and be focused in the moment. This also invites the mind to develop the next limb of yoga (dhyana/meditation), while at the same time helping us to really enjoy the scent of the flowers that bloom along our unique roads.

CHAPTER ELEVEN

DHYANA
Meditation

◆

"When meditation is mastered, the mind is unwavering like the flame of a lamp in a windless place."

—BHAGAVAD GITA, 6:19

◆

WITNESS

"Separate the mind from the body and unite it with the supreme soul. When your consciousness is free from its different states, know that to be samadhi."

—HATHA YOGA PRADIPIKA 7:3

The seventh limb of yoga is dhyana or meditation. Although dhyana is usually translated as meditation, I think a more accurate term would be 'witness' because it's through the practice of dhyana that we become a witness to what is uncovered through the concentration practices of dharana. People often think of meditation as sitting cross-legged with the eyes closed, but meditation is much more than the casual observer can see. While on the outside it can look passive, it's actually a very active practice that can be quite challenging at times.

Dhyana can be practiced in any number of physical positions. It can be done with eyes open or closed, and it can be experienced while moving the body or sitting still. In other words, there are many forms and expressions of dhyana. To limit it to a seated lotus position would be a shallow view. That would be like believing that digestion is accomplished with a fork. The fork may be what sets the process of digestion in motion, but the process itself is an internal one. Likewise, sitting with crossed legs may start the process, but the practice of dhyana is something that happens internally. And just as a fork is not the only tool used for eating, sitting with closed eyes and crossed legs is not the only position used for dhyana.

When we practice dhyana, we shift the mind out of judgment and into witnessing. In doing this we neutralize the long-held ego judgments. These ego judgments are the threads that make up the veil of maya that has been placed over our eyes. It is dhyana that removes this veil and eventually allows us to find samadhi (ecstasy).

Through the previous six limbs of the yoga practice, we've been working with the illusion. In the yamas and the niyamas we sought to modify our lives by developing a well-adjusted moral code and cultivating habits that would make space for spiritual practice. We then focused on the body through asana, pranayama and pratyahara. This allowed us to convert the ego's chief line of defense—the body—into an asset and tool. In doing this, we turned our time in the physical body into a practice of evolution. Rather than having the body used against us like a heavy anchor holding the veil of maya tightly in place, it became a grounding tool and a platform on which to build the rest of our practice. In effect we learned to use the body and its sensations to poke holes in the ego's faulty belief system.

In Chapter Ten we entered the mind and learned how to stay focused in the present moment through the practice of dharana. This allowed us to look at the mind more closely by resisting the tricks and games of the ego. Dharana is like a microscope that enables us to focus on the mental, emotional and physical seeds that bear the fruits of suffering. By bringing the mind to the present moment, dharana gives us a choice. Until we learn to practice dharana, life would seem to be a roll of the dice. When we practice dharana we recognize that we have a choice. Unfortunately, that choice is still between various forms of illusion. Without practicing the seventh limb, dhyana, we simply create a more palatable version of maya. When we practice dhyana, however, we begin to transcend the ego and dissolve the illusion of maya.

We began our exploration of yoga by looking at the concept of Atman. Atman is who each of us is, in Truth. Yet clinging to false ideas about yourself or others bends and warps our perception of who we are. This allows us to experience the ego or false self.

When we come to the present moment, we have the choice of keeping things the way they are or changing them. Changing the mind in a way that leads to a more satisfying life is not a bad idea, but it is not the goal of yoga. In fact, if we stop there we have missed the whole point. Once this choice is presented to us, yoga would have us choose to let go—to wake up.

For example, in the present moment a woman could choose to leave her husband because her relationship with him is simply not working. Making this choice may well be a good thing. But if it only serves to shift her identity from married and unsatisfied to single and searching, not much has been accomplished. She has not reached the root of the problem. By practicing dhyana she could not only choose to modify the circumstances of her life, but also forgive the judgments held on the various levels of her mind and so find a greater degree of liberation. This would be a big step in the process of transcending her ego and ending her suffering.

THE MIND

"Brahman is all, and the Self is Brahman.
This Self has four states of consciousness."
—MANUKYA UPANISHAD, 1:2

Before we can understand the practice of dhyana, we must first take a closer look at the mind. There are many models for describing the mind from Eastern, Western and psychological points of view. All of them have their merits, but all of them are necessarily limited. The mind is a vast inner realm with many nooks and crannies. To try to describe it in volumes of text would be impossible, so the few short pages that follow are only intended to point our minds in the direction of understanding. With that said, let's take a look at some of the basic components of the human mind.

As I've already stated, the mind is a vast territory with many facets. For simplicity, I usually divide the mind into four levels. There is not a well-defined line where one ends and the next begins, but to keep things simple we will speak of these layers of consciousness as distinct and separate areas.

The first is the conscious mind. We are most familiar with this level. It's here that we have our conscious thoughts and basic cognitive processes. Usually thoughts in this area take the form of words, but can also include images and visualizations. The characteristic that most defines this level of consciousness is our awareness of it. Other levels of the mind are much less accessible to most of us, so we tend to be more familiar with the conscious mind. For this reason, we identify most with the conscious mind.

When we practice dhyana, the conscious mind is the first area we encounter. Here, most of us find minds that chatter a lot. Depending on how much chatter is there, this can be a hard layer to move beyond.

In many ways, this level of the mind is like the surface of the ocean. It's greatly influenced by the winds of our external life. Sometimes the conscious mind is very choppy, while at other times it can be quite calm. Whatever the state of this first level of the mind when we enter into dhyana, the goal is to bring our awareness deeper. If we are able to maintain the focus that was developed in the last limb, dharana, it's possible to sink below the conscious mind, even during the most turbulent storm.

The second level is the semi-conscious mind. We visit this part in daydreams and during the REM stage of sleep. We're aware of this part of the mind, but only partially. Awareness of this level is usually foggy at best, and experience of it is easily forgotten. That's why it can be so hard to remember dreams after waking up.

If we're able to quiet the conscious mind, we'll find that conscious awareness moves deeper, eventually entering the semiconscious mind. It's here that we can easily get distracted in fantasy. When this happens, it's important to return to the focus point established in the previous limb. It can be very tempting to want to engage in a fantasy, but doing so will keep us stuck at this level. Only by refocusing the mind can we move on to the third level.

The third level of mind is by far the largest. It is the unconscious mind, and most of us are completely unaware of what exists there. The terrain of this level looks much different than the others, and it can be very difficult to navigate. While the conscious mind was filled with very familiar, conscious thoughts, and the semiconscious mind is filled with dream-like images, this deepest level of the mind is filled with archetypes.

Archetypes are symbols and images that are largely defined by our cultural and religious experiences. To a Hindu, these images may include a variety of gods and goddesses from that tradition. For people raised in the West, images such as those found on a tarot deck or in fairy tales may be more common. Some of these archetypes may be recognizable, and some may be very bizarre—even beyond description. That's why trying to understand these images can be so futile. These images may provide some insight in a psychotherapy session, but can be a major distraction during the practice of yoga.

If you're able to keep returning to your focus point, you can move still deeper into the mind and experience the true Self, because underneath these three basic levels of consciousness there is a fourth. For simplicity, I'll refer to it as the Source. It's important to note that all minds originate from the same source point. This point has many names originating in many cultures. A simple Western name would be God. Eastern names would include the Tao and Brahman. Albert Einstein referred to this source as the Unified Field. Whatever you call this Source, it's important to remember that it exists within every mind. For example, in the New Testament, Jesus reminds his followers, "The kingdom of God is within." (Luke 17:20)

This source point is the origin of all thought, and as we shall see in the next chapter, it's a formless thought of pure joy, bliss and love. This thought is present within you at this very moment and at every moment, though it's likely to be buried under layers of physical, emotional and psychological baggage. It is this source point that we're trying to realize when we practice yoga.

You can compare it to the light bulb in a movie projector. It shines a continuous beam of light through the lens of the mind. This light, if it were not filtered through a piece of film, would be one uninterrupted expression of bliss and joy. But because most of us hold many judgments in our minds, these judgments act like film that bends the light and creates the motion picture of our individual and collective lives. Learning to neutralize these judgments (samskaras) starts to clean up the mind, dissolve the illusion of maya and make us more loving and blissful people.

– SAMSKARAS, THE SEEDS OF KARMA –

"When all mental distractions disappear and the mind becomes one-pointed, it enters the state called samadhi."
—YOGA SUTRA 3:11

If the mind were completely empty, the Source would shine through it without obstruction. That one thought of love, peace and joy would then be manifested on the stage of maya. Life in this illusion would be a perfect expression of unconditional love.

Of course, the mind is not empty and our experience of maya can be anything but loving at times. This is because most of us hold vast numbers of samskaras.

Traditionally, samskaras are seeds of karma planted within the subtle body, particularly in the nadis and chakras. However, I prefer to think of them within the context of Western psychology, where a samskara is a judgment or a psychological attachment developed by the ego that gets filed away in one of the three levels of consciousness and held in place until it's brought to conscious awareness and neutralized.

Our perception is constructed of two basic judgments—positive and negative. We've already compared the illusion of maya to a computer simulated virtual reality. While it may appear very real, it's only a bunch of ones and zeros strung together to create a false view of ourselves and others. This may seem impossible, but if you think about it, everything you encounter is largely the product of your own preconceptions.

All day long we live in duality. We constantly affirm that, "This is good and that is bad." We call one thing pleasurable and another painful. We label and file and compartmentalize everything we see. Our behavior is directed largely to finding people who will bolster our judgments so that we can maintain them, and making enemies of those who challenge them. All this does nothing more than keep us from examining our perception of the world.

Holy wars are a perfect example of this. Rather than experience Atman in all beings, people on both sides of the battlefield find their self-definition in what they are not. They seek out people who will bolster this evaluation, create an enemy to define themselves, and allies to help them lock their perceptions into place.

It's easy to pick on the turmoil in the Middle East because it seems so absurd, but in principle we do the same thing all day long in our own lives. We have a perception, and we seek enemies and allies to help us maintain that illusion. It's all about protecting our apparent need for duality.

A samskara is like a bad investment. If you were to take all your savings and invest in a stock which was doing really poorly and which continued to decrease in value, it would be a very unwise move. Yet that's exactly what we do with our spiritual wealth when we hold onto a judgment. We make investments that drain us of life and ensure that we're tired all the time. Learning to withdraw these judgments is like reinvesting our spiritual wealth in the present moment.

It's tempting to think that samskaras are based on negative judgments alone, but this is not the case. There are really only two kinds of judgments—positive and negative. Both are samskaras, and both need to be neutralized in order to realize our True nature. For instance, many of us hold a samskara that says marriage is good and another one that says divorce is bad. Both bend and twist the light of our true nature out of shape. Both bolster the idea of a false identity, and both need to be forgiven if peace is to be found. As long as we hold the judgment that divorce is bad we will harbor negative thoughts about people—perhaps even about our selves who are divorced. Rather than see Atman, we may see less than their perfect nature.

By the same token, if you judge marriage to be a good thing, you're creating a standard which Atman now has to live up to. In effect, you're saying that you'd be more perfect than you already are if you were to get married. Of course, trying to improve on the perfect requires that we first ignore or deny perfection.

This is true of all judgments. They are created to block the flow of love through the mind. Each judgment, big or small, positive or negative, is a step away from the knowledge of the True Self. Conversely, the relinquishment of those judgments is a step closer to Self-realization.

Not all samskaras are created equal. The ego cherishes some more than others, and thus it can sometimes take years of conscious awareness before we are actually able to let them go. Other samskaras aren't that big a deal and can be transcended by simply bringing awareness to them. The trauma of stubbing your toe is probably going to be easier to deal with than the trauma of being sexually abused, but the goal is always to let them go, no matter how much we feel we need to hold on them.

I met a Trappist monk on one of my stays at a Christian monastery. Most of the monks there were in silence and had little contact with visitors. But because Brother Jacob worked in the bookshop at the monastery, he was able to speak a bit more freely with outsiders. I asked him what had made him decide to let go of the world and make what many people would think an extreme choice by becoming a monk. He shared with me a touching story that has sat with me for many years.

"When I was four," he began, "my mother died, leaving me in the care of my father. My father was not a bad man, but he had a drinking problem and a lot of the time I felt like I was left alone after my mom died. Life was not easy and I became a very bitter and angry young child. My adolescent years were marked with even more challenges.

I was arrested several times and eventually wound up in a juvenile detention center. By anyone's prediction I was not headed toward a very bright future. But I met a Catholic nun named Sister Maggie who was a volunteer at the center. She took a liking to me and always took time to visit with me. She sort of reminded me of my mother, so I liked her right away too.

I thought, in the beginning, that she was just going to push her religion on me, but she never did. The only thing she did that was different from almost everyone else I had met, was that she refused to see me as damaged goods. There was something very healing about that.

"Over the year and a half I was there," he continued, "we became good friends, and I eventually asked her to tell me about what nuns do. I think I even asked her if she missed sex. She told me a little about her beliefs, but focused on what she called her contemplative practices such as 'centering prayer'. This was strangely interesting to me, so I asked her if she would teach me. She excitedly agreed and taught me a very simple meditation technique. It was so simple that I thought it was a waste of time, but she assured me that it was very effective. I practiced each morning and afternoon as she instructed. Some days were harder than others, but I managed to stick with it. I was astounded at how deep the practice took me. Although it scared me at first, her support and encouragement made it seem okay. It brought me face to face with so much that had been buried in my unconscious. I would often encounter resentment toward my father for not being more fully there for me. I also found that I had a lot of anger at God for taking my mother from me.

"It took me several years of encountering this resentment during my contemplative practice before I was able to forgive. Surprisingly, I wasn't forgiving my father or God; I was simply choosing peace over the things I had held onto for so long. I had always believed that forgiveness was pardoning bad behavior, but through this practice I have realized that it's really nothing more than letting go of the things that I had been holding onto.

"Once I let go of some of my bitterness and anger, I started to feel peace for the first time since I was a child on my mother's lap. Sadly, Sister Maggie died of breast cancer a few years ago. I am so grateful that she taught me the most important tool a person can have in life—meditation. Shortly after Sister Maggie passed on, I decided that I wanted to devote my life to opening my mind through these contemplative practices, so I joined the Order. Some people think I am making a great sacrifice by being a monk, but from what I've seen, a life devoid of deep spiritual exploration is a much bigger sacrifice."

It amazes me that he had never studied yoga. Everything he spoke about was what I had learned to do through my yoga practice. Although he was practicing a Christian form of meditation, the principles were very much the same. By focusing the mind inward and bringing his conscious awareness deeper and deeper into the mind, Brother Jacob was able to let go of many samskaras. As urban mystics, we have the opportunity to do the same thing.

Not all our samskaras will be easy to let go and it may take years of practice. But it all starts with bringing attention to them. Through dhyana we learn how to look at attachments in the mind and move beyond them. To do this we must enter into witness consciousness.

———— WITNESS CONSCIOUSNESS ————
AND THE PRACTICE OF MEDITATION

"Select a clean spot, neither too high nor too low, and seat yourself firmly on a cloth, a deerskin, and kusha grass. Then, once seated, strive to still your thoughts. Make your mind one-pointed in meditation and your heart will be purified."
—BHAGAVAD GITA 6:11-13

The practice of dhyana can take many forms, but it almost always starts with the concentration developed in the previous limb, dharana. That is only the beginning. Dhyana moves beyond just focusing the mind—it's a disengaging of the ego, like shifting a runaway car into neutral. The ego can still rev the engines, but it has become completely benign and will eventually calm down.

There are many techniques for the practice of dhyana. Sometimes a mantra is chanted; at other times the focus is on the breath, or the attention is focused on the sensations of the body. When we practice dhyana in the context of hatha yoga we use the body and the breath a lot, but these are by no means the only ways. Whatever technique is used, the underlying practice is one of entering into what is often referred to as the witness consciousness. It's here that the power of the mind is taken back, and we begin to rise above the drama of the ego. This is where we transcend the ego and allow ourselves to be lifted to higher ground.

During one of my meditation workshops I was speaking about the importance of becoming a witness to whatever comes up. After the first meditation, one of the women in the group shared that she had a hard time letting go of an election controversy. This was when Al Gore and George W. Bush were in the midst of the infamous Florida recount to see who would be the next president. It had permeated the news and it was all anyone seemed to be talking about. She was upset by the prospect that Al Gore could win the national election and yet lose because of counting problems in one state. Even as she spoke about it I could see the tension in her face and hear a slight trembling in her voice.

"I know you're not going to like this," I told her. "But the practice here is to witness what is happening in your mind. This means acknowledging it without engaging in the drama that your mind is creating."

"That's absurd," she said in a very defensive tone. "How can you ask me to just sit back while Bush steals the election?"

"I didn't ask you to sit back. I suggested you sit up straight. I also never suggested that you couldn't get involved in the political process. All I said was that you should witness the situation. In all honesty, have you ever made an effective change in your life or in your community by being in drama?"

The struggle she encountered was one that most will meet at this level of the yoga practice. Again and again we encounter negative judgments that seem so important to hold onto. Rather than let the mind step back and simply witness, the ego tries to convince us that we need to judge and label everything.

I often use the example of Hitler. His actions and ideology are so abhorrent that he would seem to be the embodiment of evil. Yet yoga makes no room for exceptions. We need to become a witness to Hitler if we want to Self-realize. The thing to remember is that stepping back and becoming a witness doesn't mean that you condone a behavior. In fact, you may actively try to prevent what they're doing. For example, many Christians who were later thought of as saints took a stand against the Nazis when they saw the atrocities being committed against Jews and other groups. The question for the urban mystic practicing dhyana is not about what action to take, but rather about what state the mind is in. To be a witness means that you look at what is before you and you don't involve your own mind in it. To spend your life hating Hitler is to ensure that the hate he has come to represent lives on. To forgive Hitler is to break the cycle and end the war. The single most important thing we can do as individuals to ensure that another Holocaust never happens is to make our own minds holy ground rather than war-torn with thoughts of conflict. The only way to do that is to become a witness to violence rather than a mental participant in it.

The flip side of this same issue happens when the ego tries to milk positive judgments. I went on a daylong meditation retreat once and spent the whole day sitting and designing a holistic healing center in my mind. While it's a noble idea to create such a center, it is not the purpose of meditation. My ego was simply using sugar rather than battery acid to keep my mind active. The practice of dhyana would have us notice the nice thoughts without becoming engaged in them, and this can be every bit as difficult as letting go of the negative ones.

There's a Zen story about a man who wanted to learn how to meditate. He found a master to teach him to sit. After his first day of practice, he came back to the master glowing. "I can't believe how wonderful this is," he said. "I saw great visions throughout my entire sit."

The master quietly replied, "Don't worry, it will pass."

People often think that the goal of a spiritual practice is to find warm, fuzzy feelings and thoughts. This is nothing more than mental masturbation. When we enter into the witness state of mind, we witness all things, and this is as true of the things the ego deems pleasurable and nice as it is of the things that seem ugly and uncomfortable. To use our spiritual practice like a mental pleasure cruise is to ensure that we never realize the true depth of the practice.

When we're in a yoga pose we use the witness principle by holding the pose and looking at it. The temptation, of course, is to judge the pose and compare it to other people's poses. There will be some poses we'll do well, and the ego will take that for a ride. Other poses we will find more challenging, and the ego will work the mind in the opposite direction. By entering into the witness mindset, we simply observe the pose. It is neither good nor bad. Whatever emotions or thoughts come up as a result of the pose are also observed. As soon as the ego starts to tell stories about the experience, we do our best to return to the breath and the sensations, and simply witness.

This is also true of seated meditation. Observing what comes up without engaging the ego in judgment is all that's needed. By becoming the witness, we withdraw that investment in our samskaras and we turn our minds over to the gentle guidance of Spirit. As we do this our minds are healed, and the whole of humanity draws closer and closer to that time when peace is our reality in this world of maya.

– THE COLLECTIVE UNCONSCIOUSNESS –

"The flowing river is lost in the sea; the illumined sage is lost in the Self. The flowing river becomes the sea; the illumined sage has become the Self."
—MUNDAKA UPANISHAD III 2:8

In any of the workshops or classes I teach, there's always a skeptic, and my Introduction to Meditation workshop is no exception. I can always count on the class skeptic to ask the same question: "Sitting around and meditating is good, but it's not really doing anything to solve the world's problems. Don't you think our time would be better spent helping the poor or cleaning up the environment?"

Of course there is little logic in this question. Lots of people don't meditate and still don't find time to help solve the world's problems. In fact, one could argue that meditation makes a person better equipped to take on the problems of the world and thus be more effective at solving them. Gandhi is a classic example.

But dhyana offers a much greater benefit to society and to the earth than just social change. Because the practice of dhyana neutralizes thought patterns and long-held judgments in the individual, it also affects the collective unconscious. This provides far greater healing than social action alone.

The notion of a collective unconscious is nothing new. Yogis and mystics have known about it for a while, but Carl Jung popularized the idea in Western culture. The idea is simple enough—all minds are connected. In other words, if I go deep enough into my mind and you go deep enough into your mind, we will meet. I have heard this compared to the spokes of

a wheel by many teachers, most notably Marianne Williamson. Our individual conscious minds exist at the rim where they appear to be separate. But if you follow the spoke down to the center of the wheel, you see that all the spokes are connected, and the closer you get to the center the closer the spokes get together.

Not only does each of us have individual samskaras, but we also share many samskaras collectively. These collective samskaras make up social paradigms that guide the way we function as a group. Sometimes these social paradigms serve us well; at other times they can be very destructive. Some paradigms work for a while and then cease to serve us.

It's not easy to change these paradigms because it's like a democracy. In order for a real shift to occur, a majority of the people needs to let go of the old way of functioning as a society in favor of a newer and more evolved way. This restructuring of our programming can only happen one mind at a time, but when enough minds let go of their individual samskaras, a paradigm shift occurs.

I once went to hear a Bible scholar speak about how the Bible and Eastern spiritual paths, such as yoga and Buddhism, were complementary. Many of the people in the room had left their Judeo-Christian backgrounds in favor of Eastern spirituality because they viewed the Bible as patriarchal and judgmental. As this man spoke, I could see that many in the audience were getting uncomfortable. He finished by commenting on how Moses and the Buddha had a lot in common. When it came time for questions, a woman in the front row raised her hand. She was visibly upset and her voice trembled as she said, "I was raised as an Orthodox Jew. I was forced to study The Torah. It is a most hateful book, especially toward women. I can't believe you have the nerve to put Moses in the same category as Buddha."

"I can understand why you feel the way you do," he replied. "Most people don't understand how Moses could be a great spiritual leader and yet lay down a law that seems so sexist. Indeed, people from both the Christian and the Jewish traditions have used his teachings to keep women oppressed. But when we take a closer look at the way society functioned during Moses' time, we can actually start to see him as one of the first feminists. At that time, a woman was property. She could be sold or beaten without any social consequences. It was not just that she had a lesser social status, she was considered nothing more than livestock. Her father or husband could treat her as poorly as he liked. If he was tired of her, he could leave her at the side of the road with nothing, and if he should die, she would have no way to protect or care for herself. By today's standards, the Law of Moses can look very sexist, but it put in place rules that for the first time gave rights to women. A man could no longer just mistreat his wife or leave her for dead. He had to take some sort of responsibility. While this was only a small step, it was a major shift in the way things were done. Of course there are those who feel they can use the Bible to justify their degradation of women and others. This is very unfortunate, because it's really the story of social reformations, and that story continues to be written today in civil rights movements around the world."

Like Moses, we are all called upon to do our part in bringing about a collective shift. Of course social action is a great way to do this, but not much will change until we start to clear away our own samskaras. As we do this, we move our tribe closer and closer to a new level in evolution.

An example of this can be found in the story of the hundredth monkey, which is actually an illustration of human rather than animal behavior. As the story goes, a scientist was doing an experiment to see how fast a new behavior could be introduced into a tribe of monkeys. The monkeys under study lived on two islands in the South Pacific. Monkeys on both islands were given sweet potatoes to eat each day. Sweet potatoes were not native to the islands, so eating them was a new experience for the monkeys. According to most accounts, he took one monkey away from the others and taught it to wash the sweet potatoes in the ocean before eating them. Then he released the monkey back onto one of the islands and watched to see how long it would take for all the monkeys to develop the new behavior. Gradually, one monkey at a time learned the behavior. It was a slow process at first, but when a certain number of monkeys learned this new behavior (one hundred is the number usually quoted), all the monkeys on the island began to wash their sweet potatoes before eating them. This rapid change in the community's behavior happened almost overnight.

The story gets even more amazing, however. At the same time the scientist was observing the monkeys on the one island, he was also observing the monkeys on the second island nearby, using them as a control group.

They were also given sweet potatoes, but none of them were taught any special behavior. When the hundredth monkey started washing his sweet potatoes on the first island, the monkeys on the second island spontaneously started washing theirs as well.

Subsequent studies have cast doubt on the accuracy of the story as told here. However, its wide acceptance over the years suggests that it illustrates an important tenet of human behavior: our thoughts are available to all other members of our species, though people are free whether or not to think them.

This story gives us a clear incentive to practice dhyana. As we neutralize our own samskaras, we have the opportunity to be one of those first hundred monkeys. Once a certain number of us change our minds, the whole of society is swept up like a rapture. What was once held as a basic truth is now brushed aside as an old idea that no longer serves us.

It's hard to believe that the United States went to war with itself over slavery. It's such a basic notion today that slavery is unacceptable, and yet there was a time when many people were willing to fight and die to keep slavery a reality. When America's 'hundredth monkey' decided that slavery was wrong, change happened.

We have a similar shift happening today on the spiritual front. Up until a few years ago, people were content to let religious leaders and institutions tell them what to believe. Now, vast numbers of people are questioning this old paradigm and choosing a more direct approach to Spirit instead. That's why practices like yoga, Buddhist meditation and Christian Centering Prayer have been attracting people in such large numbers.

As we continue to practice dhyana and neutralize our personal samskaras, and also the cultural ones we share with our tribes, more and more often we step out of Atman's way and create space for the final limb in our mystical path—ecstasy.

CHAPTER TWELVE

SAMADHI
Ecstacy

◆

"They alone attain samadhi who are prepared to face challenge after challenge in the three stages of meditation."
—TEJABINDU UPANISHAD 1:4

◆

THE PATH SO FAR

"Success is achieved neither by wearing the right clothes nor by talking about it. Practice alone brings success.
This is the truth without doubt."
—HATHA YOGA PRADIPIKA 1:66

Up until now, most of the benefits we've experienced through our yoga practice have manifested within the context of maya. Perhaps your health has improved or your relationships have become more honest and intimate. Maybe yoga has helped you discover your calling in life and you have been able to quit your job in favor of a more satisfying occupation.

All of these benefits are wonderful, and alone they make yoga an invaluable practice. But these benefits are nothing more than pleasant side effects. Remember, as I said earlier, the goal of yoga is not more limber hamstrings or freedom from chronic pain, or even a happier life; the goal of yoga is union—the realization of Atman. This goes as far beyond mere joy and contentment as a seven course banquet goes beyond a fast-food breakfast.

Throughout this book we have repeatedly come back to the concept of Atman and focused on the realization of our identity as a child of God. Each of the preceding seven limbs has sought to bring us closer and closer to the remembrance of our true nature, and here in the eighth limb of yoga we experience Atman directly. Everything we've done up until this limb has been in preparation for it. We first prepared our lifestyles. Then we prepared our bodies and our minds. Now in the eighth limb, we let go of belief and dogma. In this limb we no longer need to have faith that Atman is our true nature, because we experience it directly.

All the other limbs had the sole purpose of purifying the mind and healing our misguided perceptions. Now that that has been accomplished, at least in part, we can sit in samadhi. Samadhi is the eighth limb of yoga. It translates as ecstasy, and with good reason. There is no experience more satisfying or fulfilling than that of samadhi. Unlike the other limbs which have specific techniques associated with them, samadhi is not something that can be cultivated. The experience of samadhi is potential in every moment. The only thing that blocks us from having this experience is the samskaras that clog the mind. Once we let go of these, the experience of samadhi is allowed to flow.

Like a dam that hems in a great river, the potential for the water to flow is always there. The water is just waiting to flow. Once the dam is released, the water does what is in its very nature. Samadhi works in the same way.

Once we let go of the samskaras that dam (pun intended) the mind, the experience of ecstasy pours through. When this happens, we are changed forever.

—————————————— **A VISIT** ——————————————

"As salt and water become one when mixed, so the unity of self and mind is called samadhi."
—HATHA YOGA PRADIPIKA 4:5

From where we are right now, samadhi can seem like a far-off pipe dream. We need only try hatha yoga and seated meditation to realize that there is a lot of cleaning up to do. So often when we sit to meditate or find ourselves on the yoga mat, we get bombarded with the samskaras of the mind and the aches and pains of the body, and we can wind up feeling worse than when we started. It's not that things are really worse—it's that the practice of yoga and seated meditation shine the light of awareness squarely on the blocks in the mind, and this can be quite uncomfortable.

Even though samadhi can seem far off, it is well within our grasp in this present moment. Reaching out and touching it is not that hard, but finding the willingness to do so can be a whole different story. As we noted in the last chapter, our attachments to our samskaras can be quite strong. In spite of this natural resistance to letting go, we do have moments of surrender when, for a variety of reasons, we're able to disengage from our samskaras and hit the psychological mute button. This allows us to pierce the veil of maya for a while and see behind the illusion. We don't need to be very evolved for this to happen. Actually, my first experience with samadhi happened quite by accident, and it was so life altering that nothing, from that point on, has ever been the same.

My adolescent years were quite turbulent, and I was very unhappy. Drug and alcohol abuse were two of several manifestations of this unhappiness, as were frequent bouts of depression. As early as age fifteen it became apparent that drugs and alcohol were a problem for me, and over the course of my high school years I tried several times to stop without much success.

This struggle continued until shortly after my eighteenth birthday. It was a cold February night in 1989. At the time I had been very depressed, and I was trying to stay clean and sober. Although I had been sober for several months, I gave in to temptation once again when a friend offered me some LSD. I took it at home, alone, just before going to bed.

The trip was not a bad one—at least not compared to others, which had conjured up some scary hallucinations. When I started to come down, however, I felt the weight of tremendous guilt beginning to bear down on me. At one point I looked at myself in the mirror and realized how much I hated what I had become.

That's when I decided to kill myself. I turned my room upside down looking for a razor blade or any sharp object. Although the trip had ended, I was still not completely sober and I was, thankfully, unable to find a blade. In frustration and utter depression, I collapsed on my bed in tears. I had experienced emotional breakdowns before, but this was a catharsis of such gigantic proportions that I could almost feel my heart stop.

It was then that I experienced samadhi. Everything stopped and I felt complete peace. It was a serenity and quiet so complete and so whole that all my pain and suffering vanished like darkness at the flick of a light switch. It was so foreign to everything I knew in my life, and yet it felt like the most natural thing in the world. I couldn't help but smile, and I felt love pour through me. It was not love for one person or a group of people— it was love for all. In addition to love, there was a timeless quality to the experience, and I couldn't say how long it lasted. I fell into a deep sleep after that and woke up with the worst hangover of my life.

That night everything changed for me. The thing I had been chasing my whole life was realized in that moment. I had tripped on acid enough to know that it wasn't a drug-induced experience. In fact, I lost almost all desire to get high after that, and I have never been high or had a drink since.

I wanted that experience again, but I didn't know where to look. I didn't even know that my experience was a spiritual one. I continued my quest for answers, but because of my negative experiences with the Catholic faith I avoided anything that looked at all like religion. Perhaps that's why yoga was so perfect for me. It didn't look or feel like the religion of my past, so I wasn't threatened. How I started yoga is another story, but I have come to believe that fate has a funny way of putting what we need in our path. Through a series of unlikely events, I found my way to a yoga class, and began my conscious journey through the eight limbs.

What happened to me that night was more Grace than anything I could have planned, and it turned my life around. Now I seek that experience on a daily basis when I come to the yoga mat or sit in stillness. I am not at a point where I can surrender as completely as I did that night, but yoga has prepared my mind for the occasions when it does happen.

There are two basic ways to achieve samadhi. The first is through catharsis. A catharsis looks a lot like a mental breakdown, and I wouldn't call it fun, having experienced it that night back in 1989. As I studied and grew spiritually, I realized that samadhi was something that was often preceded by complete and utter despair. There are countless stories of people experiencing samadhi—some who had terminal illnesses and some who were being tortured in concentration camps. They had nothing left to cling to, which allows for a state of complete surrender, and it's this surrender that opens the door.

Perhaps the most beautiful true story about this experience concerns a man called John Newton. His early life was filled with abuse and he was devastated by the loss of his mother. A series of events led him to a job as the captain of a slave ship. Most accounts of his early life show him as a hard and angry man. There are many different stories about his so-called 'great deliverance', but they follow roughly along these lines. On May 10, 1748, he was on the high seas with a shipload of slaves. A great storm hit, and he believed that he and all on board would die. Although he had never been a religious man and considered himself an atheist, he surrendered and prayed for the first time. The storm passed, and his life was spared.

He was a changed man. In the silence that followed the storm, he could hear the moaning of the slaves below deck and he was so moved by their faith and passion that he penned the words, "Amazing grace, how sweet the sound…" to the tune of their moaning. Some accounts of the story have him turning the ship around and freeing the slaves, while others have him keeping the slaves but treating them with exceptional kindness and keeping them safe in his care. In either case, he was a changed man that night and I believe he had an experience of samadhi.

Because of my 'accidental' experience with samadhi, I too was like a new person overnight. I wanted that peace and that feeling of completion again, but I didn't know how to find it. I was a bit nervous since it was only through a near fatal bout of suicidal depression that I had been able to find it up to that point. I wanted the experience again, and in my heart I knew there had to be a better way to find it. Yoga, at least for me, is that better way.

The second way we can seek out the experience is through mysticism. There are many mystical techniques that can prepare the mind for samadhi, but in this book we are focusing on yoga.

As we work our way through the eight limbs, we teach the mind how to let go and surrender the psychological, physical and emotional blocks that keep us held back in life. This process of learning to let go will sometimes give way to the experience of samadhi. Samadhi is not something you can decide to experience. It's something you experience when you allow yourself to let go of what you are not and remember your true identity as a spark of the Divine. Since that night in 1989, I have revisited the ecstasy of samadhi a dozen or more times. Most often it is during my seated meditations or on the yoga mat, but on occasion it has occurred during some other aspect of life.

In 1999, I was at the Pink Saturday celebration in San Francisco. Pink Saturday is a giant street party where thousands of LGBT people and their supporters flood the streets of the Castro—San Francisco's iconic gay neighborhood. It was a warm night, so thousands of people showed up to dance and celebrate sexual diversity.

I was supposed to be meeting my friend Jasper there, but the crowd was quite large so I knew that spotting him would not be easy. I decided to climb on top of a bus stop shelter and wait for him there. I figured I'd have a better view, and it would be fun to rise above the fray. And rather than just sit and wait, I thought I'd spend some time dancing. There was a DJ station right across the street, and she was playing some great music. At first it was a bit awkward to dance as the shelter was rounded on top and a bit slippery. I was also a bit self-conscious, being up in front of so many people. In time, though, I slipped into a relaxed dance space and enjoyed the moment. As I danced and let go more and more, I found that I slipped deeper and deeper into a trance-like state. I started to notice a pulse of energy over the crowd that connected us all like some sort of a web. It was as if we were all breathing and moving in sync.

Shortly after that, time stopped and my sense of 'me' disappeared. I realized that there was dancing happening but no dancer. There was breathing happening but no breather. I was fully in the experience, but also much bigger than the moment. It was like every particle in the universe had been arranged to make that moment one of unimaginable joy. Although there were thousands of people there, I knew them all and had a deep sense of unconditional love for every one of them.

Then I had a thought, "Wow, I'm in samadhi!" With that thought, the experience dissolved. As soon as there was an 'I' and an experience of time, I was no longer in samadhi. That's when I noticed Jasper waving to me from the ground with a few of his friends. I wasn't sure if I had been in samadhi for a few seconds or a few hours, but it reminded me that, in any moment, ecstasy is a choice.

In many ways, this brief glimpse of samadhi is like waking up for a few minutes and learning that what you were dreaming was just a dream. Although you may roll over and go back to sleep, the dream can never be the same because you know it is a dream. Through yoga practice we open ourselves to these moments of alertness, and when they happen, Truth is revealed. Once you have had the experience of samadhi, no matter how briefly, you will not be the same. Things that once seemed so important will appear meaningless, and things that once seemed like a fairy tale will more and more become your reality.

With each experience of samadhi, we are reborn. A piece of the ego is transcended and Atman is consciously realized. This is the goal of a yogi and of all true spiritual paths. By practicing the seven previous limbs frequently and consistently, this experience will manifest more and more often, and a seeker will make great strides in his or her spiritual evolution.

ENLIGHTENMENT

"For him the universe is his garment and the Lord not separate from himself. He offers no ancestral oblations; He praises nobody, blames nobody, is never dependent on anyone."
—PARAMAHANSA UPANISHAD 1:4

Although I get along quite well with my family, I think I am sometimes seen as the black sheep. The last time I was home, we were all sitting around the dinner table telling jokes and having fun. First my cousin John told a joke about two nuns. Then my brother told a joke about a guy getting involved in a bar contest. I decided to share a joke that had been floating around the yoga community in California. "What did the guru say to the hotdog vendor?" I waited for a few moments and answered, "Make me 'one with everything'." They just sat there. There was not a smile—not even a courtesy chuckle.

My brother flatly asked me, "What does stretching have to do with hotdogs?"

I explained to my family some of the basic ideas of yoga that we have been exploring in this book, and while they still didn't find the joke funny, they were interested in knowing a bit more about yoga. After my explanation, however, my brother had yet another question, "Are you 'one with everything'?"

"Yes and no," I responded. "I am one with everything, and so are you. Actually, everyone is. It's really not a question of whether a person is one with everything, because that's a given—it can never change. The real question is, 'Have I realized that I am one with everything'? In that case, my answer would have to be 'no'."

As I've just mentioned, I've had brief glimpses into samadhi, but for the most part I identify with the separateness of my ego much more often than I do with the wholeness of Atman. There are people, spiritual masters, who have let go of many of their samskaras, and they live in a state of samadhi much of the time. People like these are no different than the rest of us, but they live in a state that for us is only a potential. The key difference is that most of us live from our egos and on occasion have brief glimpses into samadhi, whereas these masters live from Spirit and briefly get deluded by maya, but quickly return.

There are many masters who have become enlightened through the practice of yoga, but yoga is not the only path. There are enlightened beings from almost every religion and culture. People like Black Elk, Buddha, and Jesus are just a few.

Unfortunately, people often turn these masters into gods and superheroes. Rather than learning to model their lives after these masters, people can easily be deluded into wanting them to save the day. It's easy to feel ourselves in free fall, like Lois Lane waiting for Superman to swoop down and catch us. This is not the goal of an enlightened master. Instead, they remind us that we have our own wings.

While these enlightened ones are not there to save the day for us, they can play an important role in our own journey to enlightenment. They can do this in several ways. First, they serve as models. How they lived their lives can be a great source of inspiration in how we structure our own lifestyles.

For example, Gandhi can serve as a great example for all of us in the way he took abuse and refused to resort to violence, but went to prison for his convictions. When life presses us and we're tempted to respond with violence, we can remember the life example of Gandhi and know that nonviolence can free us from our egos in much the same way that Gandhi's nonviolence led to the freedom of India.

Another way these masters can help us is through their teaching. Albert Einstein once said, "You cannot solve a problem with the same thinking that created it." Most of us think in constructs that the ego has created, and this is why it can be helpful to learn from a more enlightened being. We need a new way of thinking.

Since the ego is incapable of creating this new way of thinking, it can be incredibly helpful to learn from someone who is further along the path. Asking the ego to come up with an enlightened way of thinking is like asking a child if he or she wants vegetables or candy for dinner. By trusting in the knowledge and wisdom of a more enlightened person, we gain from their wisdom and create a new way of thinking for ourselves.

One of the greatest gifts a master can give is to set an example. If it were not for the great masters from both East and West who have demonstrated that enlightenment is possible, I might well have given up a long time ago. For me, the great masters act as a cheering squad as I climb my mountain. Because they have already reached the top, I know it's possible, and that I'll eventually make it.

I tend to think of enlightenment as a ripening or maturation, rather than as a goal we reach. People love to speculate about whether a teacher is enlightened or not. I prefer to see teachers as being of varying degrees of ripeness. Likewise, I tend to think of my own enlightenment as a process. In time, I'll be more enlightened. This will happen as I transcend more and more of my samskaras and allow Spirit to guide my thoughts more and more of the time. Once we let go of a large number of our samskaras, we will begin to experience that sense of oneness with everything.

To be one with everything would be to walk through life and see the interests of others as no different from your own. It would mean seeing Atman in everyone, from the homeless person to the person of an opposing political persuasion. It would mean surrendering the voice of your ego and replacing it entirely with the voice of Spirit, and it would require choosing ecstasy in each moment over the constant drama of the ego.

Enlightenment sounds like fun, and I have no doubt it would be a lot more fulfilling than the ego-driven existence where most of us live. But it means letting go of the ego identity altogether, and this is the source of our greatest fear, because it means letting go of the basic notion of good and bad.

I went to hear Marianne Williamson speak a few years ago, and one of the gentlemen in the audience shared with us that he was very afraid of becoming enlightened. She told him not to worry, because most of us are not that close. Her response was very wise, because Spirit does not cause us to become enlightened by ripping the rug out from under us. That would undermine free will. For most of us this process is a gradual awakening, with Spirit gently rocking us to a more conscious state of being.

Before we can really become enlightened, we need to look at the root of our ego's thought system. All of our samskaras are really growing from the same seed thought—duality. Duality is the idea that some things are good and others are bad. All delusion flows from this basic illusory notion. To be fully enlightened would mean that the seed of all thought would not be founded in duality, but rather in Oneness.

This way of thinking is so foreign to the duality-based thought systems most of us use, that it's hard to imagine what it would be like. In many ways the duality-based thought system and the thought system based on unity are like the Macintosh and Windows platforms on computers. While they may function in many of the same ways, their basic 'behind the scenes' programming is quite different. That's why you can't run programs designed for Macintosh on Windows and vice versa.

Most of us experience life through the eyes of duality, and that's where Spirit meets us—to teach us unity. Yoga teaches us to let go of our dualistic judgments one by one, until the step from the old way of being to the new way of being is easy and painless. It's a self-defeating idea to worry about our own or another's level of enlightenment. It only serves to distract us from the task at hand—forgiveness in the present moment.

Enlightenment is inevitable. It will happen as surely as the sun will rise. But in the world of time it may take many years or lifetimes. The only way to speed up this process is to practice the eight limbs of yoga or some other form of mysticism. By working the eight limbs of yoga into all of life, we reduce our suffering and draw the mind closer and closer to that day when samadhi will be the norm, and ego drama will be nothing more than a minor distraction.

-THE CONSCIOUS EXIT—MAHASAMADHI-

"In the supreme climax of samadhi they realize the presence of the Lord within their heart. Freed from impurities, they pass forever beyond birth and death."
—SHVETASHVATARA UPANISHAD 2:15

When I first moved to San Francisco, I felt a strong calling to work with people who were in the advanced stages of AIDS. At the time high doses of AZT were still being used, and the death toll was mounting daily. The obituaries were many pages long each week, and there was a general sense of despair on the streets. I had seen the reports in the papers and I had lost some friends back east, but I was not prepared for what I was walking into.

Shortly after arriving in California, I met a man on the bus. We had a nice conversation, which eventually led to his asking my occupation. I told him I was a massage therapist and a yoga teacher and that I had just moved to the city to see if I could make a difference in the AIDS crisis. He told me of a friend of his who was very sick and wanted to get regular bodywork in these waning days of his life. Although I didn't like the idea of doing house calls with my big, heavy, massage table, the man seemed so concerned for his friend that I felt this was something I needed to do.

When I first met his friend, I was taken aback to see just how unhealthy he was. He was so frail that I was almost afraid of breaking him as I moved my hands over his body. I had worked on many people who were sick, but never on someone this close to death. I tried to avoid the subject of his mortality so as not to upset him, but that seemed to build a deafening tension. I guess he could feel the tension too, because he said something that sliced right through it.

"If you have any questions, it's okay to ask," he said.

"I don't think I have any questions, I replied. "You were very honest on your medical history form."

"Not about my medical history—about death. I know you can see it. I am leaving soon. If you have any questions, I would like to talk with you about it."

I didn't know what to say. It felt like we were going into that forbidden area where few dare to tread—as uncomfortable as standing at the urinal when the guy next to you starts up a conversation.

"I don't know what to say. I'm sad that this is happening to you. I wish I could do more to help you."

"Well, you could spend a little extra time massaging my feet," he joked. "This curse is really a gift, and it took all of this to make me realize it. I never knew a person could be this sick. Believe it or not,

I was very healthy and attractive once. Now I can hardly get out of bed and I'm covered with sores. Up until a few weeks ago I was so angry. Everything I had ever loved was taken from me—my health, my good looks, and the closet full of expensive clothes that no longer fit me. Even the BMW, which I just finished paying for last year, sits in the garage and collects dust. It seemed so unfair that my life is being demolished by a tiny bug that I can't even see. "Something changed a few weeks ago though," he continued. "I've never been one to go to church or pray, but the situation seemed to call for it. Of course, I was hoping for one of those miracle cures that you read about in Reader's Digest while sitting on the toilet, but, as you can see, I didn't get better. A miracle did happen that day though—an even bigger one. In that moment, I let go of my fighting and my clinging to all the unimportant things that have plagued my life. Everything I had clung to my whole life—even my very identity—meant nothing when I let go. In that release I found peace; I am now ready to go home. My mother is coming up to visit next month. I'm just waiting to see her. She's very old and is having her own share of problems, but she's going to fly up from San Diego. I just want to sit with her and have tea. She was raised in England, and tea is a big deal to her. Once I do that, I'll be ready."

I was massaging his back as he told me this, and I was grateful his face was down in the cradle, because I was embarrassed by the tears that I had to keep brushing back. At first I was crying for him. It's not easy to see someone who is dying, but as he spoke, the tears were as much for myself as for him. I had sought through my yoga practice for years to find the peace that he had found, but was only able to experience it in fleeting glimpses. My prayer that day was that I would be able to know his peace before I left this world.

I continued to work with him until the end, and I met his mother when she came to visit. Shortly after that he passed on. Even though I went to him with the intention of helping him find peace, I now believe it was he who helped me learn a great lesson about the final stage in a yogi's life— mahasamadhi.

Mahasamadhi is a conscious exit from the body at death. It's more than simply dying, for we will all do that and usually have little choice as to when. Mahasamadhi is about consciously letting go of everything and moving into the next realm with a clean slate.

The fear of death seems very natural, but this is one of the best examples of the ego's upside down perception of the world. Death is the most natural thing there is, and to fear it is no more logical than to fear sunsets. Like the sunset that is sure to follow the sunrise, death is the natural result of birth. Resisting it and clinging to life only serves to hold us back while we're here and prevents us from living life to the fullest.

It's important to note the difference between the natural instinct for survival, and an ego-based fear of death. Wanting to maintain a healthy and long life is natural and logical. While we're here, we have lessons we need to learn, and that won't be possible if we play in traffic or drink window cleaner. On the other hand, the ego's obsession with youth and longevity are great barriers to our spiritual evolution.

For many of us, death is not an easy subject. Because our egos so closely identify with the body, death can be a very fearful thing. The practice of yoga is based on the idea that we are not our egos, but rather the eternal Atman. Once Atman is realized, there is no cause to fear death or to speak about it in whispers.

As we have noted so many times, Atman—the essence of who we are-- is eternal. Atman is the soul; it was not created at birth and does not die at death. Only the form a soul takes can change. If we resist that change, we suffer, and there is no change bigger than physical death.

Many yogis believe in reincarnation. Others believe in an afterlife such as the one depicted in Western belief systems. Still others see the human soul dissolving back into a great source. While reincarnation is the belief that is traditionally associated with yoga, it is by no means the only way of viewing the afterlife. In my opinion, any belief that reminds us of the eternal nature of the soul is helpful.

Through the practice of yoga, we prepare ourselves to exit the body in a conscious and enlightened way. This allows the moment of death to be a liberating time that lets us move on. Rather than a time of fighting and clinging, it becomes a time of freedom and celebration.

None of us knows when we will be called home. None of us knows when the accident is going to hit, or when disease is going to render the body uninhabitable. Therefore, it's important to attempt to make every moment a conscious one. In doing this we simultaneously create full and rich lives and make a clear space for entering into mahasamadhi.

As long as we are in a body, we will have some sense of separation. Even the most enlightened people need to maintain some sense of 'me' to function in this world of form. Mahasamadhi, then, is the final step a yogi takes to free the mind from the insanity of the ego. Once this is done, the mind passes from the state of duality to a state of union, which is what yoga is all about.

CONCLUSION
the Dance of Yoga

"You have dispelled my doubts and delusions,
and I understand through your grace.
My faith is firm now, and I will do your will."

—BHAGAVAD GITA 18:73

"That yogi quickly attains the most beautiful practice who
everyday has conviction in his learning, conviction in his guru,
conviction in his self, and awakening of his mind."

—HATHA YOGA PRADIPIKA 7:2

Once there was a high school custodian named Joshua Joshua was a good man and all the teachers, students and parents liked him. He took pride in his work, and kept the school in tiptop shape. Joshua was content with his job, but had always dreamed of opening a small produce stand.

Although Joshua was very wise and compassionate, he could not read or write. This had always held him back in life to some extent, but he always seemed to manage. After much deliberation, the board of education passed a law that required all school employees to be able to read and write, so Joshua was let go. He was given severance pay and sent on his way.

While Joshua may not have been able to read and write, he did have a great attitude toward life. Rather than get depressed about his situation, he took his severance pay and invested it in the produce stand that he had dreamt about for so long. His dream took off and soon he was selling enough fresh produce each day to open a second and a third stand in the neighboring towns. Certainly, it was more than he could have hoped for.

Just after opening his third stand, his brother came to visit. He was quite impressed with the small empire his sibling had created and inquired what he was doing with all his money.

"I keep it all in a shoebox under my bed." Joshua replied.

"You must be kidding," the brother said. "At the very least you should keep your money in a savings account. They are free at almost any bank."

Joshua agreed, and took his shoebox full of money to the bank the next day. Of course the bank manager was eager to help him, but was a bit perplexed as to how a person would come across a shoebox full of money. So Joshua told his story to the bank manager.

"That's amazing—you're living your dream, and we're glad to have you as a member of our bank. All I need you to do is sign this form for me, and you'll have your account."

"I'm sorry," Joshua said. "I can't read or write."

The bank manager was in awe. "You have done so much—can you imagine where you would be if you could?"

Joshua smiled thoughtfully and said, "I'd probably still be cleaning toilets."

This story has been told by many people, and passed around the internet with many variations. I wish I knew to whom I should give credit because this story speaks volumes about the concepts we've been exploring in this book.

Unlike Joshua, most of us resist change in our lives until the pain of not changing gets too great. Joshua waited until the Universe gave him the nudge to move on to higher ground and then took bold steps.

For many of us, it's an aching body or a stressed-out mind that brings us to the yoga mat. This can seem like a bad thing in the beginning, but it's really a cleverly hidden gift. Whatever it is that gets us to the practice of yoga, it is only the excuse that Spirit uses to get us started on the path.

Yoga has a wonderful way of taking our greatest weaknesses and turning them into our greatest spiritual assets. At first we learn to do this on the yoga mat with poses that challenge us physically, mentally and emotionally. But when we open the heart and mind to yoga, it becomes so much more. The poses of life soon become our practice too, and we have one opportunity after another to practice yoga all day long in our busy urban lives.

Ultimately, the eight limbs of yoga become like an eight-step dance, where each situation and relationship in which we find ourselves become our dancing partners. We begin our dance by finding our moral ground with the yamas and then move on to the next step— cultivating a healthier life through the niyamas. Through asana and pranayama we take the next two steps in our dance by coming more fully into the body. Pratyahara, the fifth step, brings us to the realm of the mind through the doorway of the senses, and the sixth step, dharana, grounds us in the present moment. The seventh step in this mystical dance, dhyana, allows us to witness our dancing partner, and the last step, samadhi allows us to find ecstasy in the experience.

At first it's not easy to learn this eight-step dance, and we can feel like we have two left feet on the dance floor of life. But as we mentioned in the beginning, yoga is a practice. As we practice this dance and use these principles, we will respond to life more and more easily. As we do this, life will look less and less like a slam dance and more and more like an elegant waltz.

Through this practice, our modern urban lives can be powerful and mystical experiences, filled with all the wonder and magic that was once reserved for those living as monks and nuns. By using the practice of yoga in this new way, we have the opportunity to see the world with new eyes and find joy in each step of the journey. We will learn to welcome the difficult poses that life presents to us, and not to attach ourselves to the ones that come more easily.

By working this ancient practice in a modern way, every breath can be a practice of mindfulness that gives way to unimaginable joy. This is the practice of yoga—this is the path of the urban mystic.

GLOSSARY

Ahimsa—The practice of nonviolence. One of the five yamas outlined by Patanjali in his Yoga Sutra.

Ajna—The sixth major chakra, located at the eyebrows in the front of the body and at the back of the head. The seat of intuition, perception and cognition.

Amrit Desai—The founder of Kripalu Yoga and Amrit Yoga.

Anahata—The fourth major chakra, located at the breastbone in the front of the body and between the shoulder blades in the back. The seat of love and compassion.

Analome Valome—A breathing technique using alternate nostrils combined with counting and holding the breath.

Apana—The downward breath or exhalation.

Aparigraha—The practice of greedlessness or nongrasping. One of the five yamas outlined by Patanjali in his Yoga Sutra.

Archetypes—Symbols and images held in the unconscious mind. They are usually based on cultural images or symbols, and make up the samskaras in the unconscious mind.

Arjuna—One of the central figures in the Bhagavad Gita. As a great warrior, he finds himself in the middle of a great battlefield. Krishna appears to him and teaches him about Spirit.

Asana—Literally 'to sit', but often translated as pose. The third limb outlined by Patanjali in his Yoga Sutra.

Ashtanga—Eight limbs. Any style of yoga that follows the eight limbs outlined by Patanjali in his Yoga Sutra. See also Ashtanga Vinyasa.

Ashtanga Vinyasa—Often called 'Ashtanga Yoga' or 'Power Yoga', this style of yoga was developed by Sri K. Pattabhi Jois and is characterized by a set sequence of poses connected with vinyasa (flowing movement).

Asteya—The practice of nonstealing. One of the five yamas outlined by Patanjali in his Yoga Sutra.

Atman—The True nature within all beings. The expression of the Divine. The eternal, unchanging and all knowing part of the being. Also called the Soul, Self, Higher Self and True Self.

Aura—The energy field in and around a living being's physical body.

Austerity—See tapas.

Autobiography of a Yogi—The life story of Paramahansa Yogananda, one of the first yogis to come to the West from India. It has become a classic text for many modern yogis.

Autonomic nervous system (ANS)—The branch of the nervous system that governs unconscious activities such as digestion, heart rate and immune functioning.

Aversion—One of the two ways the ego keeps the mind in a state of outward projection. See also craving.

B.C.E.—Before Common Era. B.C. (Before Christ) used to be the standard way of dating events that happened before the birth of Jesus about 2000 years ago. Because the calendar is shared by both Christians and non-Christians, the dates traditionally ending in B.C. have been changed to B.C.E. See also C.E.

Bandha—Literally, 'bond' or 'bondage', but most often translated as 'lock.' There are three locks in the human body which section off the three cavities (abdominal, thoracic and cranial). They are used by a yogi to regulate the flow of prana throughout the body, to aid in breath retention and to bring stability during asana (poses). The three bandhas are mula bandha (root lock) located at the pelvic floor or perineum, uddiyana bandha (abdominal lock) located at the diaphragm, and jalandhara bandha (throat lock) located at the throat and hyoid bone.

Bhagavad Gita—One of the great spiritual texts to come out of India. It is believed to have been written about 2,500 years ago, around 500 B.C.E., and is part of the epic Mahabharata. It is the account of Krishna's spiritual wisdom as it was given to his student Arjuna. See also, Krishna and Arjuna.

Bikram Yoga—a style of yoga practiced in a heated room.

Black Elk—A Native American elder.

Brahmacharya—The practice of moderating one's sexual energy. One of the five yamas outlined by Patanjali in his Yoga Sutra.

Brahman—The Formless expression of the Divine. The ultimate reality beyond any idea of time and space.

Brahma—Part of the Hindu Trinity. God in the role of creator. See also Shiva and Vishnu.

Breath—See Pranayama.

Breath of Fire—See Kapalabhati Pranayama.

Buddha, Gautama—The founder of Buddhism who lived around 500 BCE.

Catharsis—A complete mental and emotional breaking down that gives way to a new and more evolved way of thinking and a release on a mental, emotional and energetic level.

C.E.—Common Era—A.D. (Year of our Lord) used to be the standard way of dating events that happened after the birth of Jesus about 2000 years ago. Because the calendar is shared by both Christians and non-Christians, the dates traditionally ending in A.D. have been changed to C.E. See also B.C.E.

Centering Prayer—A form of Christian meditation.

Central nervous system (CNS)—The system in the body that controls body functions on both a conscious and an unconscious level. Chakras—A spinning energy vortex in the subtle body. Although the human body has many of these energy centers, there are seven major chakras located along the spine. Each one is responsible for various physical, emotional and mental aspects of life.

Choudhury, Bikram—The founder of Bikram Yoga and Bikram's Yoga College of India.

Christian Trinity—In Christian theology, God is one being in three forms. The Father, the Son and the Holy Spirit (Holy Ghost).

Collective Unconscious—The part of the unconscious mind that we all share. Because all minds are connected, a change in one mind affects the collective unconscious and is shared by all.

Concentration—See dharana.

Conscious Mind—The part of the mind of which we are consciously aware.

Contentment—See samtosha.

Craving—One of the two ways the ego keeps the mind in a state of outward projection. See also aversion.

Darshan—Wisdom given from guru to disciple, usually in the form of a talk or discourse.

Death—See mahasamadhi.

Dharana—The practice of concentration. The sixth limb outlined by Patanjali in his Yoga Sutra.

Dhyana—the practice of meditation or witnessing. The seventh limb outlined by Patanjali in his Yoga Sutra.

Dirga Pranayama—'The complete breath.' A breathing technique in which the lungs are used at their capacity in an effort to draw in a large amount of prana.

Ecstasy—See samadhi.

Ego—The small self. The part of the mind that believes it is separate, finite, limited and defined by external things, rather than simply being. Energy—See prana.

Energy Pathways—See nadis.

Enlightenment—A state in which all or most samskaras have been neutralized, and a person exists in a state of pure joy and bliss. See also samadhi.

Evolution—The natural course by which the universe discovers itself. The speed of this process can be greatly accelerated through mystical practices such as yoga.

Fight or Flight—See sympathetic nervous system.

Focus Point—An object on which to focus the mind during the practice of dharana. Oftentimes the breath, a mantra or a phrase from a sacred text.

Gandhi, Mohandas K.—One of the great modern spiritual and political leaders to come out of India. By promoting nonviolence, he was able to free India from the British Empire. He was assassinated in 1948.

God—A generic term used to describe Spirit in its many forms.

Gospel—One of the four books (Matthew, Mark, Luke and John) in the New Testament that chronicle the life and teachings of Jesus of Nazareth. There are other books such as the Gospel of Thomas, which offer a similar account, but are not included in the traditional Christian Bible.

Greedlessness—See aparigraha.

Guru—Usually translated as teacher, though the literal meaning is 'from darkness to light.' A guru, therefore, is one who helps lead a spiritual seeker from the darkness of the ego to the Light of Atman.

Gyatri Mantra—One of the oldest and most famous mantras in India. Hatha Yoga—Any style of yoga that is focused primarily on poses (asana) and breathing (pranayama). Most of the styles of yoga taught in the West are forms of hatha yoga.

Hatha Yoga Pradipika—A sacred text written by the sage Svatmarama. Although it is fairly new compared to other texts (about 1400 CE), it is considered the basic text on the practice of hatha yoga.

Hinduism—The largest religion of India. Although yoga and Hinduism are different, they share some of the same historical roots, as well as several sacred texts.

Hindu Trinity—In Hindu theology, God is thought to have three basic forms in this world: Brahma (the creator), Vishnu (the sustainer) and Shiva (the transformer).

Ida—One of the two main energy pathways that wrap around the central energy column that runs through the spine (sushumna). See also pingala.

Illusion—See maya.

Intoxicants—Things that intoxicate, such as alcohol, recreational drugs, and nicotine.

Integral Yoga—A devotional style of hatha yoga developed by Swami Satchidananda.

Ishvara—One of the Hindu gods, often referred to as 'the Lord of Yoga.'

Ishvara pranidhana—The practice of surrender to a higher power. One of the five niyamas outlined by Patanjali in his Yoga Sutra. Iyengar Yoga—A style of hatha yoga that focuses on proper alignment and frequently uses props.

Iyengar, B.K.S—The founder of Iyengar Yoga.

Jesus—The central figure in Christian theology. Believed by many Christians to be the Son of God, and believed by many yogis to be a great teacher and skilled yogi.

Jois, Sri K. Pattabhi—The founder of Ashtanga Vinyasa yoga. See also Ashtanga Vinyasa.

Kabala—A form of Jewish mysticism.

Kapalabhati pranayama—A form of breathing that involves pumping the diaphragm and expelling the air forcefully. Sometimes called 'Breath of Fire' or 'Skull Polishing Breath.'

Karma—The universal law of cause and effect.

Karma yoga—The practice of serving others while seeking to relinquish the ego judgments projected by one's own ego.

Kirtan—A traditional style of Indian chanting, which starts off slowly and increases in tempo. Often accompanied by dancing and celebration.

Kripalvanandj, Swami Shri—One of the great modern yogis, and the person for whom the Kripalu style of yoga was named.

Kripalu—A style of yoga that focuses on body awareness. This style of yoga is often taught in three stages. Stage one is a willful physical practice used to open the body and prepare the energy pathways (nadis). Stage two is a practice of will and surrender in which poses are held for longer periods of time, and stage three is a practice of total surrender into a free flow that is guided by the movement of one's life force (prana). Sometimes called 'Meditation in Motion.'

Kripalu Center—The largest yoga ashram in the United States. While the focus at this center is Kripalu Yoga, it has become an eclectic center offering many styles of yoga and meditation.

Krishna—A great teacher from Ancient India, and one of the central figures in the Bhagavad Gita.

Kumbhaka—Breath retention. Holding the breath in or out.

Kundalini—See kundalini-shakti.

Kundalini-shakti—The coil of energy that, when in a dormant state, lies at the base of the spine and climbs up the spinal column (sushumna) during a kundalini experience or during sexual arousal. This energy will become active naturally from time to time, but can be stimulated through various yoga practices or through shaktipat. See also shaktipat.

Loincloth—A white cloth wrapped around the waist. The traditional attire for yogis who had renounced the world and given up worldly possessions.

Mahasamadhi—A conscious exit from the body at physical death.

Manipura—The third major chakra, located just above the navel in the front of the body and in the upper part of the low back. The seat of personal identity, will, and individuality.

Mantra—A word or phrase that is repeated over and over as part of a spiritual practice.

Maya—The collective illusion that all beings share before they achieve Self-realization. The illusion that the physical universe is real and exists within time and space.

Meditation—The practice of quieting the mind and listening to the voice of Spirit (the Sadguru). See also dhyana.

Mind—The cause of all experience on the physical, emotional and mental levels. The mind is usually seen as having different levels, which include the conscious, unconscious and semi-conscious. From a yogic point of view all minds originate from one source (Brahman).

Moral Restraints, The—See yamas.

Mudra—The literal translation is 'seal.' Mudras are gestures or movements within the yoga practice, such as dhyana mudra, which is the act of resting the hands in the lap, right hand in the left, with thumbs touching.

Muktananda, Swami—The founder of Siddha Yoga.

Muladhara—The first major chakra, located at base of the spine. The seat of physical survival and tribal (cultural) consciousness.

Mystic—One who seeks a direct experience of the Divine through various forms of meditation.

Nadi shuddhi—A cleansing or purification of the energy pathways in the body (nadis).

Nadis—The energy pathways that carry prana (life force) throughout the body. They are often referred to as 'subtle nerves' and there are said to be at least 72,000 of them in the human body.

Native American spirituality—A general term used to describe the earth-based spiritual practices of the tribal people who originally inhabited North, Central and South America. Practices and beliefs vary from tribe to tribe.

Namasté—A Sanskrit salutation that is often offered between yogis. It means, "The Light in me acknowledges the Light in you."

Niyamas—The second limb of yoga outlined by Patanjali in the Yoga

Sutra—This second limb is made up of five observances that are designed to cultivate a lifestyle and attitude that is conducive to spiritual practice. See also shauca (purity), samtosha (contentment), tapas (austerity), svadhyaya (study), and ishvara pranidhana (surrender).

Nonstealing—See asteya. Nonviolence—See ahimsa.

Observances—See niyama

Om—Sound of creation. The seed sound and vibration from which all matter springs forth. Often chanted as part of a yoga or meditation practice.

Original Sin—A belief that each soul is born into this world with imperfection (sin) as its basic nature, and that spiritual salvation is needed in order for it to enter the Kingdom of Heaven in the afterlife. Although this belief is shared by most Christian denominations, the concept does not appear in the Bible and only surfaced in Christian doctrine around 500 CE. This concept is completely reversed in yogic thinking where the soul is seen as innately perfect and good, and only a mistaken identity (ego) creates suffering. Therefore, a yogi seeks a realization of his or her true nature rather than spiritual salvation.

Parasympathetic nervous system (PNS)—The part of the autonomic nervous system (ANS) that regulates such functions as digestion, elimination and immune functioning. Often called 'rest and digest.'

Patanjali—An Indian sage who lived around 1,000 CE and who is believed to be the author of the Yoga Sutra.

Perception—The result of taking sensory information and filtering it through the ego, resulting in a distorted understanding of Truth.

Pingala—One of the two main energy pathways that wrap around the central energy column which runs through the spine (sushumna). See also ida.

Prana—The life force that exists within all living things. This force is dynamic and flowing. When this flow is blocked or slowed, disease and dysfunction occur.

Pranayama—The practice of regulating the breath to effect a change in the body and mind. The fourth limb outlined by Patanjali in his Yoga Sutra.

Pratyahara—The practice of withdrawing the senses. The fifth limb outlined by Patanjali in his Yoga Sutra.

Puja—The daily devotions or worship offered to God.

Purity—See shauca.

Rest and Digest—See parasympathetic nervous system. Restorative Yoga—A gentle style of yoga that uses props and longer holdings to help the body find a natural state of healing and balance.

Sacred Texts—Books from any religion or culture that seem to live and grow with a spiritual seeker. Yoga draws largely from the Yoga Sutra, the Upanishad and the Bhagavad Gita.

Sadguru—The universal teacher who exists within all beings. The voice of guidance.

Sahasrara—The seventh major chakra, located at the crown of the head. The seat of spiritual pursuits and a person's connection to a higher power.

Samadhi—The experience of ecstasy. The eighth limb outlined by Patanjali in his Yoga Sutra.

Samskaras—The seeds of karma that exist in the nadis and chakras. From a Western psychological model, they are the positive and negative judgments that create and support the illusion of maya and an individual ego.

Samtosha—The practice of contentment. One of the five niyamas outlined by Patanjali in his Yoga Sutra.

Sanskrit—The language of yoga and the root of many Eastern languages. Although still spoken, it is primarily used for science and ritual.

Satchidananda, Swami—The founder of Integral Yoga and the Yogaville Ashram.

Satya—The practice of truthfulness. One of the five yamas outlined by Patanjali in his Yoga Sutra.

Self, the—See Atman.

Self-realization—See enlightenment.

Self-study—See svadhyaya.

Semi-conscious mind—The aspect of the mind of which we are only partially aware, such as in daydreams, and the dreams experienced during REM sleep.

Sexual moderation—See brahmacharya.

Shakti—Consort of Shiva. Also, Spirit taking form in matter. Often associated with kundalini-shakti at the base of the spine.

Shaktipat—The process by which a guru or more evolved teacher wakes the kundalini energy in his or her student or devotee. This can be done through touch, chanting, a look, or distantly, through a prayer-like gesture.

Shauca—The practice of cultivating purity in the mind, diet and life. One of the five niyamas outlined by Patanjali in his Yoga Sutra.

Shishya—A guru's student or disciple.

Shiva—Part of the Hindu Trinity. God in the role of destroyer and transformer. See also Brahma and Vishnu.

Siddha Yoga—A devotional style of yoga that is known for its use of chanting.

Sit—See asana.

Source—See God and Brahman. Spark of the Divine—See Atman. Spirit—See Sadguru.

Subtle Body—The energy body made up of nadis and chakras. The subtle body would also include energetic systems from other traditions such as acupuncture meridians and auras.

Suffering—The end result of living in delusion (maya) and the perceptions of the ego.

Surrender—See ishvara pranidhana.

Sushumna—The primary nadi (energy pathway) in the human body that runs through the spine. It is from the sushumna that all other nadis originate.

Svadhisthana—The second major chakra, located just below the navel and in the low back region. The seat of sexuality, creativity, and procreation.

Svadhyaya—The practice of study, both self-exploration and the study of sacred texts. One of the five niyamas outlined by Patanjali in his Yoga Sutra.

Svatmarama—The author of the Hatha Yoga Pradipika and the father of all modern forms of hatha (physical) yoga. It is believed that he lived during the 14th century C.E.

Swami—A term of respect meaning 'one with Self.' It also refers to an ancient monastic order.

Sympathetic nervous system (SNS)—The part of the autonomic nervous system (ANS) that governs emergency situations on an unconscious level. Things like blood pressure, adrenaline and heart rate are all controlled by this aspect of the ANS. Often referred to as 'fight or flight.'

Tapas—The practice of cultivating a simple and austere life. One of the five niyamas outlined by Patanjali in his Yoga Sutra.

Ten Commandments—The basic moral code outlined by Moses in the book of Exodus. The moral foundation for most Christian and Jews.

Torah, The—The first five books in the Jewish Bible—generally believed to have been written by Moses.

Truth—When spelled with an upper case 'T', the ultimate reality that lies behind all perception. When spelled with a lower case 't', a statement that is accurate and based on fact.

Truthfulness—See satya.

Ujjayi pranayama—A basic breathing technique that focuses the breath and creates an ocean-like sound in the throat.

Unconscious mind—The deepest part of the mind of which most people are unaware. For most, this unexplored part of the mind is the largest part of the psyche.

Unified field—In the field of physics, the source point. See also God.

Upanishads—A collection of short sacred texts from India that are frequently bound together in one larger book.

Urban mystic—A term used to describe a new type of spiritual seeker who lives in the world, and practices yoga, meditation and other techniques that were traditionally reserved for people who had left the world to live in solitude or in monasteries.

Vishnu—Part of the Hindu Trinity. God in the role of sustainer. See also Shiva and Brahma.

Visshudha—The fifth major chakra, located at the throat and back of the neck. The communication and communion centers.

Wicca—An ancient earth-based religion that originated in Europe and focuses on the cycles of the moon and sun.

Witness Consciousness—The practice of stepping back and observing a situation rather than engaging in ego-based drama.

Yama—The first limb of yoga outlined by Patanjali in the Yoga Sutra. This first limb is made up of five moral precepts that are designed to cultivate a lifestyle and attitude that is conducive to spiritual practice. See also ahimsa (nonviolence), satya (truthfulness), asteya (nonstealing), brahmacharya (sexual moderation), and aparigraha (greedlessness).

Yoga—A 5,000-year-old practice that seeks to unite the soul with the creator. Literally translated as 'yoke' or 'union', yoga seeks to unite which is perceived to be separate.

Yoga poses—See asana.

Yoga Sutra—One of the basic texts from India, written by Patanjali. The foundation for most modern forms of yoga.

Yogananda, Paramahansa—The author of the classic yoga book, Autobiography of a Yogi, and the founder of Self-Realization Fellowship.

Yogi—One whose primary spiritual path is yoga.

Yogini—The traditional term for a female yogi. Most women no longer use this term and simply use the term yogi, which was originally used to describe men only.

APPENDIX A:
THE SEVEN CHAKRAS

Chakra 1 | Muladhara: Survival, tribal consciousness

Chakra 2 | Svadhisthana: Sexuality, procreation, partnership

Chakra 3 | Manipura: Personal power, individuality

Chakra 4 | Anahata: Love and compassion

Chakra 5 | Visshudha: Communion, communication

Chakra 6 | Ajna: Perception, intuition, cognition

Chakra 7 | Sahasrara: Connection to Spirit

APPENDIX B: THE EIGHT LIMBS OF YOGA

1. **Yama | Restraint**
   - Ahimsa-Non-harming
   - Satya-Truthfulness
   - Asteya-Non-stealing
   - Brahmacharya-Sexual Moderation
   - Aparigraha-Greedlessness

2. **Niyama | Observance**
   - Shauca-Purity
   - Samtosha-Contentment
   - Tapas-Austerity (Simple Living)
   - Svadhyaya-Study (Self Inquiry)
   - Ishvara Pranidhana-Surrender

3. **Asana | Sit (Pose)**

4. **Pranayama | Breath Regulation**

5. **Pratyahara | Withdrawal of Senses**

6. **Dharana | Concentration**

7. **Dhyana | Meditation (Witness)**

8. **Samadhi | Ecstasy (Liberation)**

APPENDIX C: HISTORY OF YOGA

4,000–2,000 BCE

Pre-Vedic Period—Archeological evidence on clay tablets depicting person seated in a yoga position.

2,000–1,000 BCE

Vedic Period—First references to yoga found. Mostly references to breath control.

1000–500BCE

Pre-Classical Yoga—The earliest Upanishads are written with many more references to yoga. Still no hard and fast philosophy or practice established.

500 BCE

Epic Period—Books like the Mahabharata and Bhagavad Gita, and later Upanishads are penned. Yoga as its own distinct practice begins to take shape and form.

200 CE

Classical Period—Patanjali writes the Yoga Sutra (including the eight limbs). This becomes the backbone of most modern forms of yoga, including most styles of hatha yoga popular in the West.

500 CE–1900 CE

Post Classical Yoga—Many styles of yoga emerge based on various elements of the Yoga Sutra and the eight limbs. Hatha yoga begins to form and the basic poses get established. The Hatha Yoga Pradipika is written around 1400 CE by Svatmarama Yogi.

1900-CE to present

Modern Yoga—Various masters come to the United States and other western countries and begin teaching yoga to a new audience. Hatha yoga is greatly influenced by the gymnastics of the British empire and hybrid vinyasa styles of yoga are born out of British occupation of India.

The Future of Yoga

No one knows what will happen with yoga's future, but many scholars and advanced yoga teachers believe a new wave in the 'yoga craze' will involve the more spiritual and philosophical aspects of yoga.

APPENDIX D: THE SACRED TEXTS

The Vedas

The Vedas are the oldest sacred texts from India, dating back about four millennia. They also provide the first record of yoga philosophy (though it is faint). There are four main Vedas: Rig, Atharva, Sama, and Yajur, each written largely as hymns, invocations and prayers to nature deities. The Rishis (ancient Indian mystics) are thought to have orally composed them in the area that is now Kashmir. The Vedas are considered by Hindus to be a direct revelation from God (Shruti).

The Upanishads

The word Upanishad means, "to sit down near (the teacher)." The oldest Upanishads were orally composed as early as 1000 BCE and the newest were penned later than 1900 CE.

The Upanishads pick up where the Vedas left off and most are considered to be direct revelation from God (Shruti) as well. The Upanishads have many more references to yoga but again mostly in the realm of philosophy. According to tradition, there are 108 different books, but more than 200 have been counted.

Unlike the Vedas, the Upanishads contain more practical wisdom on aspects of daily life. Both the yogic and Vedanta philosophies draw from these texts, as does the Hindu faith.

The Bhagavad Gita

The Bhagavad Gita is part of the larger epic work called the Mahabharata, which is the mythical and historical account of the founding of India. In the Bhagavad Gita, Krishna (the teacher) appears to Arjuna (the student) and teaches him the principles of yoga as a means to end suffering.

The story takes place during a great battle, which is a metaphor for the internal battle that Arjuna himself is experiencing as he is about to engage in battle against his kinsmen. The various sides are believed to represent the deep split in Arjuna's mind among family, religion, personal will, and moral duty (dharma). The bulk of the Bhagavad Gita is a Q&A session between student and teacher.

The Yoga Sutra

The Yoga Sutra was written between 200 BCE and 200 CE and the author (or the editor) is believed to be Patanjali. The word sutra means 'thread' and the Yoga Sutra are aphorisms that are threaded or woven together to create the rich tapestry of yoga philosophy.

There are 195 sutras (aphorisms) in total, divided into four sections. The eight limbs of yoga (Ashtanga Yoga) come from the second chapter of the Yoga Sutra.

Hatha Yoga Pradipika

Just as the Yoga Sutra codified yoga in a way that gave yoga philosophy more structure, a yogi by the name of Svatmarama codified the physical practice of hatha yoga in his book, Hatha Yoga Pradipika (Light on the Forceful Yoga). It is believed to have been composed sometime in the 14th century CE.

In this book he begins the journey to what we think of today as hatha yoga. Though not easy to read, and still looking very different from the yoga many of us know today, the Hatha Yoga Pradipika addresses familiar concepts such as basic forms of breath control (pranayama), basic poses (asana), cleansing techniques (kriya), locks (bandhas), hand and body gestures (mudras), and a number of other concepts fundamental to most styles of hatha yoga.

Gheranda Samhita

This book followed the Hatha Yoga Pradipika and was penned sometime around 1700 CE. Like the Pradipika, it is very different from the hatha yoga practiced today, but it does introduce about 25 additional poses and several concepts not present in the earlier Pradipika.

The Shiva Samhita

A text that followed the Hatha Yoga Pradipika and the Gheranda Samhita and was written around 1800 CE. The Shiva Samhita deals more with the energy anatomy of yoga and includes information on the mudras, breath work, and additional yoga poses.

RESOURCES FOR THE URBAN MYSTIC

DarrenMain.com
Learn more about Darren's classes, workshops, retreats, online events, video courses and trainings and find a treasure-trove of inspiring free resources.

FREE DOWNLOAD
The Urban Mystic Study Guide

Host an Event
If you run a yoga studio, company or nonprofit organization, Darren is available to offer workshop, trainings and talks. Learn more about hosting an event or scheduling an online talk at Darren's website.

DarrenMain.com

Books By Darren

If you enjoyed *Yoga and the Path of the Urban Mystic*, be sure to check out Darren's other books available in Paperback, ebook and audiobook formats.

The River of Wisdom: 108 Life-Changing Reflections

Inner Tranquility: A Guide to Seated Meditation

The Yogi Entrepreneur:
A Guide to Earning a Mindful Living Through Yoga

Spiritual Journeys along the Yellow Brick Road

Hearts & Minds: Talking to Christians about Homosexuality

Social Media for Teachers and Healers: The Essential Guide to Growing Your Following without Losing Your Zen

Available on Amazon and Audible

Darren's Books

ACKNOWLEDGEMENTS

Special thanks to my Family:

My son Jaden Patrick Main. I now realize that everything in my life—the joy, the pain, the spiritual practice, was all to prepare me for being a daddy. For as hard as it is to be a single father, greeting each morning with one of your 'snuggle hugs' makes the job seem easy. In your eyes I have found my dharma and your laughter is the fastest path I have found to samadahi.

My mother Kathy Ascare, My father John Main, My brother Jason Main and my sister Jennifer Main. "Auntie" Wanda Pierce, My nieces Zoe Main, Haley Holdridge, Lauren & Emma Glazer and my nephews, Chase, Jake and Tyler Flynn, Preston, Wyatt, Don, Amy, Alden, Leigh, Josie, Joe, John, Sarah, Peter, Linda, Kate. Adelina, Arthur and Mary, and all the Mains who are too numerous to mention.

Special thanks to my Sadhana brothers and sisters:

All of my students and teachers have been my greatest asset as I have walked the path of the Urban Mystic. Although I would like to acknowledge you all, my publisher wouldn't hear of it. There are a few folks who have touched my yoga practice so deeply that I want to mention them here.

The Yoga Tree, YogaWorks, CorePower and Yoga on the Labyrinth communities. Sue Louiseau, Patrick Finerty, Michael Lynch, Christopher Love, Jasper Trout, Danni Pomplun, Michael Watson, Jacki, Carlose, Kristi, Peter and Jimmy, Nicholas Lizza, Kimberly Wilson, Aaron Star, Peter Wong and the amazing community at Grace Cathedral including

Ramona Draeger, Jude Harmon, Bishop Marc Andrus, Malcolm Young and all of the other clergy, staff and volunteers who work tirelessly to support the Yoga on the Labyrinth community. An EXTRA special thanks to Ellie Brown for introducing me to the path of yoga.

Special thanks to my Editors:

Sue Louiseau, I want to thank you most of all. Your passion for this book kept me going, and your hours of editing, coordinating, photocopying, and dealing with Sanskrit made this book possible. Thank you for letting the Sadguru flow through your editing pen. I would also like to thank: Patrick Finerty, Keith Perry, Betsy Haggerty, Mia Masia, Deborah Muir, Ellyn Shea, Michael Newman, Nathan Williams, and Kim Hedges. You've all made great contributions to this book, and it has been so much fun to get to know each of you through your comments and critiques.

Made in United States
North Haven, CT
03 August 2022

22166795R00164